Staff Retention in African Universities and Links with Diaspora Study

By

Paschal Mihyo
Organization for Social Science Research in
Eastern and Southern Africa
P.O. Box 31971
Addis Ababa
Ethiopia

ISBN: 987-99-8858-942-5

Printed by
QualiType Ltd., Accra. Tel: 325266-9

Table of Contents

List of Boxes and Tables v
List of Abbreviations vi
Preface viii
Acknowledgment xi
Executive Summary xii

1.0. **Introduction** 1
1.1. Methodology 2

2.0. **A Decade of Innovative Reforms in African Tertiary Education Institutions** 3
2.1. Innovations in Management, Curriculum and Delivery 4
2.2. Organisational and Financial Reforms 7

3.0. **Staff Capacity Erosion as a Threat to Innovative Reforms: Systemic Issues** 9
3.1. Brain Drain, Brain Exchange and Brain Gain 11
3.2. Systemic Issues at Regional and National Levels that Encourage Brain Drain in HEIs 13
3.2.1. The Policy Framework 13
3.2.2. Policy Implementation Capacity Deficits 19
3.2.3. Funding Formulae & Statistics 22
3.2.4. The Regulatory Framework 25

4.0. **Management Issues that Undermine Reform Efforts & Lead to Staff Losses** 26
4.1. Infrastructure 27
4.2. Quality of Students 28
4.3. The Management of Research & Staff Advancement 30
4.4. Job Satisfaction & the Management of Perceptions 33

5.0. **The Motivation Revolution in African Institutions of Higher Education** 36
5.1. Innovative Ways of Retaining Staff at the Kwame Nkrumah University of Science and Technology in Ghana 36
5.2. The New Salary and Incentive Schemes at the University of Zambia 38

5.3   Measures Aimed at Retaining Staff at the University of Cape Coast,
        Ghana   39
5.4   An Integrated Approach to Motivation at the Ghana Institute of
        Management & Public Administration   40
5.5.   Staff Views on Strategies for Enhancing Staff Retention   41

6.0.   Redressing the Brain Drain   43
6.1.   State Support for Economic Growth   43
6.2.   Promoting Peace, Security and Stability   45
6.3.   Investing More in Education   45
6.4.   Creating Capacity to Learn within Higher Education Institutions   46
6.5.   Improving the Quality of Education& Creating an Educated
        Workforce   47
6.6.   Supporting Returnee Programmes   48
6.6.1. The Experience of TOKTEN and RQAN   48
6.6.2. MIDA in Ghana   49

7.0.   Linking up with the Diaspora   50
7.1.   The South African Network of Skills Abroad by UCT   53
7.2.   The South African Diaspora Network: Founded by UCT   53
7.3.   Linkages with Experts and Academics in the Diaspora   54
7.4.   Global Educational Initiative for Nigeria   54

8.0.   Linking up With Other Global Knowledge Networks   56
8.1.   The Global Development Network   56
8.2.   The Fulbright Fellowship Programme   57
8.3.   Global Networks of Mathematicians in Africa & the Diaspora   59

9.0.   Conclusions   60

10. 0. Recommendations   61
10.1.   Recommendations to Higher Education Institutions   61
10.2.   Recommendations to National Authorities   62
10.3.   Recommendations to Regional & International Development Partners   63

References   64

Annex 1:   Officials Interviewed   70

List of Boxes and Tables

Box 1:   Academic Staff Views on Why UNZA Loses Staff   29

Box 2:   Reasons for Loss of Staff at the National University of Rwanda
According to Interviewed Staff   31

Box 3:   Why Universities Still Lose Staff   35

Table 1:   UNZA New Salary and Benefit Scheme of 2007   38

Table 2:   Fulbright Fellows of African Origin 1999-2007 by Disciplines   58

Table 3:   Regional Distribution of Top Black Mathematicians
Registered by American Mathematics Society, 2007   59

Abbreviations

AAPAM	African Association for Public Administration and Management
AAU	Association of African Universities
AU	African Union
ACTS	African Centre for Technology Studies
ADEA	Association for the Development of Education in Africa
ADEA-WGHE	ADEA Working Group on Higher Education
AERC	African Economic Research Consortium
ATPS	African Technology Policy Studies Network
AVU	African Virtual University
CERGE	Eastern European Economic Research Institutes Network
CODESRIA	Council for Development and Social Science Research in Africa
EADN	East Asian Development Network
ECA	Economic Commission for Africa
EERC	Economic Education Research Consortium
EFA	Education For All
ERF	Economic Research Foundation
EUDN	European Development Research Network
GEIFON	Global Education Initiative for Nigeria
GIMPA	Ghana Institute of Management and Public Administration
GMPs	Ghanaian Migrant Professors
GTZ	German Agency for Technical Cooperation
HEIs	Higher Education Institutions
ICT	Information and Communication Technology
IOM	International Organization for Migration
IT	Information Technology
IUC	Inter University Council
KIST	Kigali Institute of Science and Technology and Management
KNUST	Kwame Nkrumah University of Science and Technology
LEAD	Linkages with Experts and Academics in the Diaspora
MIDA	Migration for Development in Africa
NUR	National University of Rwanda
OAU	Organization for African Unity
ODN	Organization for Development Research Network
OECD	Organization for Economic Cooperation and Development
OSSREA	Organization for Social Sciences Research in Eastern Africa
PMO	Prime Minister's Office
RQAN	Return of Qualified African Nationals
RECAAST	Regional College of Applied Arts, Science and Technology
SANEI	South Asian Network for Economic Research Institutes
SANSA	South African Network of Skills Abroad

SARIMA	Southern African Research in Management Association
SARUA	Southern African Region Universities Association
SIDA	Swedish International Development Agency
TCC	Technology Consultancy Centre
TOKTEN	Transfer of Knowledge Through Expatriate Nationals
UK	United Kingdom
UN	United Nations
UN-PAARD	UN Programme of Action for Africa's Economic Recovery
UNDP	United Nations Development Programme
UNESCO	United Nations Educational Scientific and Cultural Organization
UNICEF	United Nations International Children's Fund
US	United States
UCT	University of Cape Town
VC	Vice Chancellor
VILP-IBRO	Visiting Lecture Team Programme-International Research Organization
WARIMA	West African Research in Management Association

Preface

A quick glance at the growth and poverty reduction strategies in Africa, commonly known as Poverty Reduction Strategies (PRS), indicates a few points of strength and weakness. The strong points are that they are very clear on the causes of poverty and they analyse very well the weaknesses of the institutions supposed to implement, monitor and evaluate policies. They cluster the major areas of intervention in what are referred to as 'pillars' of the policies. In the majority of these policies, it is acknowledged that while the countries are resource rich, they have serious capacity problems that curtail their capability to maximise benefits arising out of their resources. Serious lack of capacity in key areas on production services and governance is raised as the main cause of the continent's entrapment, and while African countries are not short of pro-poor policies, policy analysis, coordination, implementation, monitoring and evaluation are severely constrained. The major weakness of the PRS documents, however is that in spite of the articulate analysis of these capacity gaps, they propose solutions that are very unlikely to solve these problems to fill the gaps.

While most of the capacity gaps require highly skilled specialists to design and implement policies, develop products and provide services that are capable of meeting the needs of the people, the development of such skills does not feature prominently in these strategies. In this lies the major paradox of the poverty reduction and national growth strategies. They are bold on the problem and shy about the appropriate solution. Most of them put a lot of emphasis on increasing primary school enrolment, and while mention is made here and there of secondary education, tertiary education is addressed very hastily and abandoned very quickly. Recently, in the measurement of progress made on PRS and the Millennium Development Goals (MDGs), experts had put a lot of efforts in the search for correlations between primarily school and enrolment and poverty, in general, and employment in particular, although most of them know that no country has ever developed or leapfrogged any development process only because it produced many primary school graduates. Expecting to address health, food insecurity, environmental and other issues or to mount industrialisation and agricultural transformation programmes without addressing issues of higher education, in general and capacity for policy management, science and technology in particularly, is to expect something that has never happened anywhere else to happen to Africa.

Among other interventions, strengthening higher education in strategic areas such as engineering, medicine, biotechnology, law, economics, public policy management, social policy and other areas holds the master key to new avenues for Africa's development. Therefore, tertiary education, from teacher training to vocation and university education, is critical to the attainment of the PRS and

MDGs. In spite of their importance in the anti-poverty formula, tertiary education institutions are experiencing financial and ecological stress. Most of them, while set up to accommodate on tenth of their current student populations, lack teaching facilities and are losing staff due to poor remuneration and internal governance problems. In trying to resolve some of these problems, the majority have embarked on reforms that involve commercialisation of services, privatisation of facilities and vocationalisation of curriculum. On the side of academic staff, the struggle to make ends meet has forced many to engage in what Professor Kenneth King recently referred to as the *juakalification* (moonlighting, which is known in Kenya as 'jua kali').

Given the capacity erosion that has characterised these institutions over the last three decades, it is not surprising that they are not taken seriously in the search for solutions to the cycles of poverty on the continent. However, the few organisations that see their potential for transforming themselves and the continent, have not given up hope that given the necessary recognition and support, adequate investments in tertiary education in Africa can lift the continent out of its present levels of poverty and marginalisation. Among those organisation are the African Union that has now strengthened its higher education division and launched new initiatives on revitalising higher education; the African Development Bank that has launched a programme on Higher Education Science and Technology and Vocational Education and Training (HESTVET) to boost science, research and innovation in its member countries; the Africa Capacity Building Foundation (ACBF) that funds and coordinates a network of post-graduate training institutions under its partnership training institutions and New Partnership for Africa's Development (NEPAD) that has developed a higher programme for sustained growth.

Building on these regional initiatives, the Association for the Development of Education in Africa (ADEA) has continued its efforts to support education in Africa in a holistic way, starting from early childhood development to higher education. In 2004, it supported the Association of African Universities to undertake a comprehensive study on higher education innovations in Africa, with specific reference to universities, with a view to identifying their innovation programmes as they attempt to emerge out a long-term financial and related crisis. The Staff Retention and Diaspora Study, commissioned by ADEA's Working Group on Higher Education (WGHE), is a follow up to the 2004 Innovations Study. It focuses on issues of capacity erosion and strategies for staff retention in a selected number of universities and examines the innovative ways in which these universities are trying to limit the damage caused by brain drain and staff losses. It also looks at the contribution that developing links with the African Diaspora can make to the minimisation of problems caused by the brain drain. The findings were presented at the ADEA Biennial Conference held in February 2008 in Maputo, where it was also agreed to have a follow-up programme.

The ADEA Working Group on Higher Education is pleased to be able to share the results of this study, with the hope that through this effort, the crisis of staff erosion in African tertiary education institutions will be brought to light and higher education given more space in poverty reduction strategies and in the implementation of MDGs.

Goolam Mohamedbai
Secretary General
Association of African Universities

Acknowledgement

The ADEA Working Group on Higher Education would like to express its appreciation for the support and efforts that were invested by various institutions and individuals in the preparations of this report. The successful completion of the research and the report could not have been possible without the relentless efforts of the consultant, Professor Paschal Mhiyo, who in 12 days, managed to travel to four countries and produced the first draft in less than two months. During the research, the study benefited immensely from the cooperation and support of the following persons, to whom we are immensely grateful. Professor Agyeman Badu, Deputy Rector , Ghana Institute of Management and Public Administration (GIMPA); Mr. Gerard Nyabutsisti, Deputy Rector, Finance and Administration, Kigali Institute of Science, Technology and Management; Professor Kwasi Adarkwa, Vice Chancellor, Kwame Nkrumah University of Science and Technology (KNUST); Professor W. Ellis of KNUST; Professor Silas Lwakwbamba, Rector, National University of Rwanda, (NUR); Professor Addow-Obeng, Vice Chancellor of the University Cape Coast; Professor Eric Danquah, University of Ghana International Programmes Directorate; Professor Lante Lawson, Provost, University of Ghana Medical School. Professor Nii Otu Nartey, University of Ghana Dental College; Professor Stephen Simukandga, Vice Chancellor, University of Zambia and Dr. A. Ng'andu, Registrar, University of Zambia. There are many officials who participated in interviews in these institutions, who though not listed, their contributions are highly appreciated and acknowledged. Finally, this report could not have seen the light of day without the tireless efforts and facilitation of Mrs. Alice Sena Lamptey, Coordinator, ADEA-WGHE and Ms. Annick Agbotame, Assistant Project Officer, ADEA-WGHE.

Executive Summary

Objectives
The Association for the Development of Education in Africa (ADEA) Working Group on Higher Education commissioned this study with the objective of examining the issue of staff retention in African institutions of higher education and the contribution that can be made by the Diaspora in reducing the effects of brain drain in these institutions.

Methodology
Four countries were chosen for the study: Ghana, Nigeria, Rwanda and Zambia representing the three sub-regions and two of the four official languages of the AU. Given the size of Nigeria and the numbers of higher education institutions in that country, a separate study was carried out for that country, whose findings are referred to in this report. An open questionnaire was used, supplemented by documentary survey and participant observation.

Innovations in Higher Education Institutions
Between 1995 and 2005, some institutions of higher education in Africa undertook fundamental institutional and curriculum reforms.
- They have adopted new management techniques including development of strategic plans.
- There has been a re-design of curriculum to make it more demand-oriented.
- Most of them have adopted new and alternative methods of delivery, including the use of new information technology.
- There has been more collaborative teaching and research programmes within and across borders.
- Some have decentralised their systems of governance and organised mergers of higher education institutions.
- All of them are engaged in the search for new sources of finances.
- The majority have taken steps to strengthen private-public partnerships in the delivery of services within these institutions.

Systemic and Management Constraints to Reforms
The main obstacle to these reforms is staff capacity erosion in these institutions, and it is aggravated by the following factors:

- African governments do not have proper channels for coordinating government policies on staffing issues in knowledge institutions.
- Regional policies aimed a strengthening higher education institutions in the past were not adequately implemented due to low capacity for policy formulation, analysis and implementation.

- There is a big wage gap between the majority of African countries and developed countries and this keeps pushing skilled people out of the continent.
- Frameworks that regulate higher education institutions lack consistency and unity of purpose.
- Very few countries have a funding formula for higher education that captures all the functions and activities of higher education institutions.
- Systems of data and information management in institutions of higher education and their regulatory agencies are weak and this makes it difficult to give adequate support to higher education institutions.
- There is unregulated competition between institutions of higher education in some countries and over-regulation of these institutions in other countries. The former creates unfair competition, while the latter stifles any competition at all.
- Low quality of students, lack of teaching facilities and resources, low support for teaching and poor accommodation facilities de-motivate academic staff.
- Lack of support for research and rigid or over-centralised promotion procedures inhibit staff advancement and encourage turnover.
- Perceptions that there is no distributive justice, fairness or respect for individual or group rights can undermine job satisfaction and lead to turnover.

Innovative Motivation Systems in Selected Institutions

In coping with labour market competition within their countries and abroad, several higher education institutions have reviewed their salary and benefit schemes. They have adopted new incentive schemes that seek to raise the standards of living of their staff. However, some of these changes are, or will soon be, overtaken by changes in incentive and payment schemes of their competitors in other sectors or countries. Interviewed members of staff think that if motivation strategies are to be effective the following points ought to be considered.

- Higher education institutions should be supported to pay enabling salaries to staff with which basic, health and schooling needs of their children can be met.
- Loan guarantee schemes that can enable staff to acquire respectable shelter and means of transport need to be developed.
- Employees should be enabled to enter private pension and health insurance schemes that can give adequate support to their needs.
- Reward and recognition systems need to be decentralised to be meaningful.
- Without increased funding for research, promotion and advancement will remain based on arbitrary criteria.
- Tertiary institutions need to lobby governments and donors for more support for teaching, research and office accommodation facilities.
- Further inter-university networking may reduce staffing problems.

Redressing the brain drain

To reverse brain drain in Africa, there is a need for partners in development to join forces and create conditions for sustained economic growth that can enable governments to support all sectors, including higher education and honour their international obligations including the right to education, health and a decent income for their citizens; invest in infrastructure; promote peace, stability and security to reduce the problem of involuntary migration and attract those abroad to return; invest in education at all levels to enhance the quality of education; support HEIs to support other sectors of the economy and establish lifelong learning systems and innovations and technology learning institutions and create conditions that can enable those in the Diaspora to come back.

Linking Up with Global and Regional Knowledge Networks

To reduce staff retention constraints, there is need for tertiary education institutions to link up with existing global and regional knowledge intensive networks in a more structured way, preferably through the ADEA, AAU and sub-regional higher education bodies. Some of these networks have been active in African academia for decades and if structural links are strengthened, their role could be further enhanced. They include:

- The *Global Development Network* with 3700 experts worldwide in 90 countries, a portfolio of US$20million for competitive research, postgraduate training and five global centres of excellence including the African Economic Research Consortium.
- The *Fulbright Fellowship Programme* that sent 279 scholars of African origin to African universities in 32 countries from the US over the period 1999-2007 and supports many African academicians for postgraduate training in the US.
- The *Global Networks of Black Mathematicians* in general and women black mathematicians in particular, most of them based in Africa, North America and Europe.

In addition to these global initiatives, there is growing awareness that Diaspora resources are ready and available to team up with African intellectuals to make a value added contribution to development initiatives on the continent. To tap these resources, some African universities and their regulatory agencies have initiated programmes to link up African tertiary education institutions with the Diaspora. These initiatives should be nurtured, supported and emulated by others.

Recommendations

A. Recommendations to higher education institutions
Strengthening teaching and learning
   a.   Strengthen internal quality assurance systems through self assessment, peer review, and regular voluntary programme accreditation;

b. Introduce customer surveys, student involvement in evaluation of courses and ensure customer follow-up;

c. Institutionalise customer or stakeholder contact through focus groups in key institutions, listed contacts and electronic feedback mechanisms; and

d. Introduce academic quality guarantees and spot-check procedures and enforcement mechanisms, sanctions and rewards.

Improving research management

a. Develop long-term research programmes on issues relevant to national development programmes and long-term national development visions and goals;

b. Strengthen partnerships with governments and the private sector;

c. Increase inter-faculty, multi-disciplinary collaborative research; and

d. Increase transparency in programmes and resources accruing from research and technical advisory services.

Staff recruitment and advancement

a. Devolve recruitment and promotion procedures to colleges and faculties, while retaining quality control functions at the centre; and

b. Shorten time taken in decision-making on recruitment and promotion in the context of competition for skills within and outside national borders.

Diversifying financial resources

a. Enter into partnerships with private sector for research and provision of services;

b. Increase earnings from research contracts from private sector and governments;

c. Negotiate franchises with state owned enterprises for product development and service provision;

d. Commercialise innovations and intellectual property arising out of research; and

e. Strengthen statistical and data systems and develop quantitative and qualitative norms for inputs, outputs and outcomes in all core activities.

Linking with the Diaspora

a. Establish or strengthen links with alumni within and outside the country and establish databases on their areas of specialisation;

b. Identify areas where the Diaspora can have a value-added contribution to make; and

c. Develop joint programmes with Diaspora organisations for funding and support for Diaspora involvement in selected areas.

B. Recommendations to national authorities

- Increase training on higher education management, quality assurance and leadership for change management in higher education institutions and support education reforms.
- Develop norm-based funding formulae for all education sectors.
- Upgrade norms for quality assessment in all sectors of education.
- Address factors that affect the quality of education at all levels.
- Develop sound systems for managing statistics, data and information on education sectors especially higher education.
- Decentralise decision making on staff travel, recruitment and promotion to institutions of higher education to reduce delays or loss of staff caused by lengthy procedures.
- Reduce bottlenecks on education staff travel, visa and employment permits within the region.
- Negotiate with developed countries for restriction of recruitment in sectors at risk in African countries such as health and education.
- Develop codes of conduct on foreign recruitment in sectors at risk within national borders.
- Encourage voluntary codes of social responsibility for multinational corporations and foreign higher education bodies operating within national borders on recruitment and transfer of staff to home countries or offices in other countries or regions.
- Increase public awareness about the role the Diaspora can play in revitalising higher education and the African economies and develop systems to support the involvement of the Diaspora in this process.
- Improve capacity for implementing regional and international commitments

C. Recommendations to regional bodies and international development partners

- Improve coordination of support and interventions by working through a few designated bodies at regional level thereby reducing duplication of efforts and maximising outcomes.
- Develop a division of tasks that ensures each actor specialises in an area that matches their experience and interests to avoid concentration in same areas and neglect of others.
- Combine efforts to ensure the enforcement of codes of conduct developed by the EU and several OECD countries restricting recruitment in sectors at risk in developing countries.
- Support the development of capacity for policy management, analysis, implementation and innovation at national and regional levels.
- Develop common frameworks on funding research, including promoting demand driven research programmes, reducing support for individualised research and promoting transparency and accountability for research results and outcomes.

- Support sandwich staff development programmes in order to strengthen capacity for local training and making training and research more relevant to the region.
- Intensify support for IT and computer-based research and teaching methods in African HEIs.

STAFF RETENTION AND LINKS WITH DIASPORA STUDY

1.0. Introduction

This study was commissioned by the ADEA Working Group on Higher Education. It was a follow-up study on the one carried out by the ADEA WGHE in 2004 on innovations in higher education in Africa (AAU 2004). The 2004 study was both extensive and intensive. It covered 56 higher education institutions in Southern Africa, 44 in Eastern Africa, 38 in francophone African countries and all HIEs in Ghana. Although not all these institutions managed to supply the study team with all the required information, the report documented all the major innovations that had taken place in the institutions surveyed. This study is not as intensive or as extensive as that of 2004. Its objectives are to examine the problem of staff capacity erosion in African institutions of tertiary education, find out creative and innovative strategies that have been adopted by some of these institutions to confront this challenge and suggest strategies that may be used to reduce staff losses, including the possibilities of using links with the Diaspora to widen the human resources base for the HIEs in Africa. The preliminary findings were presented at the Conference of Vice Chancellors, Rectors and Presidents of African universities at their conference in Tripoli, Libya 23-25 October, 2007. The final report will be presented to the ADEA Biennial Conference in Maputo, Mozambique in May 2008.

In order to carry out the study and within the limitations of time, four countries were chosen in which a selected number of institutions were covered. The countries chosen were Nigeria, Ghana, Rwanda and Zambia. Given the size of Nigeria, the number of universities there and the distinct role played by the National Universities Commission of Nigeria in addressing issues of staff retention and collaboration with the Diaspora in recent years, a separate study on Nigeria was commissioned by the ADEA Working Group on Higher Education and conducted by the National Universities Commission of Nigeria. Some of the findings of that study are referred to in this report especially in the section on linking with global knowledge networks, part 8. Therefore this report covers mainly three countries, although it includes the experiences of as many tertiary education institutions as possible on the continent. The efforts and initiatives of the institutions visited in the three countries are used together with others, only as case studies. It is important to point out from the onset that given the limitations of space, not all the very interesting experiences of all institutions visited are directly documented. However, most of them have been captured in the discussions.

The report starts with a review of institutional and curriculum innovations undertaken by tertiary institutions in Africa generally in the last decade. Then it examines staff capacity erosion as a factor that threatens to reduce the impact of these reforms and innovations, the systemic and management factors that encourage this capacity erosion, creative and innovative measures that have been taken by selected institutions to stem the tide and what staff and management in some tertiary education institutions say about ways and means to strengthen capacity for staff retention in their institutions. The report winds up with a discussion of strategies to redress the brain drain and improve conditions for attracting and retaining capacity staff retention within Africa, in general, and HIEs, in particular.

1.1. Methodology

The study was mostly based on the survey of published information on staff retention and the Diaspora and other global knowledge intensive networks and resources. It was supplemented by visits to the three countries as aforesaid. The time available for the field visits was only 10 days. Therefore, choice of countries to visit and institutions within those countries were determined by several factors. First, it was agreed with the sponsors that at least three of the five sub-regions of the AAU have to be included. The choice was Central Africa represented by Rwanda, West Africa represented by Ghana and Southern Africa represented by Zambia. The second consideration was that the countries chosen should represent at least two of four official languages of the AU. Ghana and Zambia are Anglophone and Rwanda is officially francophone, but in practice bilingual. A separate study was conducted on Nigeria as aforementioned.

While in Ghana, it was not possible to visit all the universities. Interviews were conducted by telephone for the University of Cape Coast and Kwame Nkrumah University of Science and Technology, while meetings were organised with officials at the Ghana Institute of Public Management and Administration and the University of Ghana. In Rwanda, meetings were held with officials at the Kigali Institute of Science, Technology and Management and the National University of Rwanda and in Zambia, only officials of the University of Zambia could be met. It was not possible to meet or interview officials of the Copperbelt University. However, for all the institutions except for the Copperbelt University, a questionnaire was administered either by telephone or at the meetings.

The questionnaire used was open ended raising key issues on staffing levels, staff turnover trends, motivation strategies and experiences with Diaspora links. It was divided into two parts. The first part with 12 questions raised issues about loss of staff before 1980, between 1980 and 2000 and after the year 2000 by faculty or discipline and the categories of staff that left employment in technical and administrative services. The aim was to establish trends of staff turnover in the contexts of economic crises and reforms in Africa. A specific question was raised on the stated or suspected reasons for their leaving employment. The second set of questions related to the number of staff that returned to the institutions especially after the beginning of economic and organisational reforms in each country by faculties and administrative departments. A third set of questions related to measures taken by the relevant HIEs to ensure that staff is retained. The second part of the questionnaire had 10 questions relating to working with professionals in the Diaspora - if they had links with them and how they were organised; who paid for the collaboration and what were the results of the cooperation.

Because the questionnaire was administered either by telephone or through face-to-face interviews, the response was 100%. Some of the questions required details that were supplied later by e-mail. The interviews with individual academic staff met were informal and not based on a written questionnaire. They were used to solicit responses on the reasons for staff leaving and what could be done to reduce turnover. These meetings were social and held in the evenings. Most of those interviewed requested that their names should not be included on the list of interviewees. Although their views were pertinent and relevant, their numbers were so small (averagely three in each institution) that they could not be taken as a representative sample of all staff.

2.0. A Decade of Innovative Reforms in African Tertiary Education Institutions

African institutions of higher education have gone through three major phases in their history. In the first phase of their formation mainly in the sixties and early seventies for the majority, they went through a period of institution building, establishing faculties, directorate and centres. During this period, their student intakes and staff numbers were small; governments were enthusiastic about their role; they had very few if any conflicts with their governments; they enjoyed adequate international support and their funding was relatively adequate. In the second phase from the mid-seventies to late eighties, they experienced rapid expansion, got frequently involved in conflicts with their governments, international support declined, student numbers increased, facilities deteriorated and staff turnover became a serious problem to their sustainability. Beginning 1990 up to the end of the millennium, economic reforms began in several countries accompanied by political and organisational changes. Donor agencies that had turned their back on higher education on the continent began re-examining their positions and committing themselves to its support. A good number of governments in Africa changed their policies on higher education, initiated education reforms, formed ministries of higher education, science and technology, relaxed control over HIEs, liberalised the delivery of education services and encouraged IHEs to undertake institutional and curriculum reforms.

Within the third phase, the period between 1995 and 2005 was the most critical. After suffering decades of neglect and financial stress, these institutions grabbed the opportunities that were offered by these changes at national and global level to re-assert themselves, recapture the initiative and restore their dignity. They undertook far reaching institutional and curriculum reforms, mostly on their own with limited support from the Association of African Universities and donor agencies. Unlike the study carried out by the ADEA Working Group on Higher Education in 2003-2004 as mentioned earlier, this one is a follow-up, and indicated that universities across four sub-regions of the continent instituted innovative changes in six key areas of governance, curriculum and delivery (AAU: 2004: 31-35).[1]

2.1.   Innovations in Management, Curriculum and Delivery

The 2004 ADEA Study covered more than one hundred HEIs on the African continent excluding those in Northern Africa. It noted major changes in the areas of governance, management and curriculum. First, the majority of universities covered in the study have embraced strategic planning. This has involved the development of strategic plans in which they have defined their mission, vision and goals and identified key activities that they are going to undertake to increase relevance, outreach, research output, quality and financial resources.[2] In most of these plans, improvement of the quality of education, mobilising resources for research and publications, staff development and enhancement of staff welfare feature prominently. Second, almost all those institutions surveyed have engaged in curriculum reforms that have seen the inclusion of new demand-oriented and needs-driven courses, while at the same time, major changes have taken place in the area of development studies shaking off the baggage of the cold war and addressing new issues such as gender, environment, human rights, conflict and poverty.[3] Third, most of the tertiary institutions of higher education that have established links with the African Virtual University (AVU) and other virtual learning networks have not

---

[1] There are five regions: Northern, West, Central, Eastern and Southern Africa. The study did not cover countries in the Northern region.
[2] Some of the most interesting among others are the strategic plans of the University of Mauritius, University of Namibia and Makerere University all of which are posted on their websites.
[3] The Institutes of Development Studies at Universities of Dar Es Salaam and University of Nairobi and the curricula of various faculties of the University for Development Studies in Ghana have been very drastically changed to accommodate new development issues.

only managed to increase their capacity to deliver distance learning courses within their countries, but they have also developed networking relations within the region and with other universities in other countries such as Australia, the United Kingdom and the United States of America only to mention a few.[4]

The fourth major change has been in the area of collaboration between African institutions of tertiary education. Led by the Association of African Universities and supported by ADEA, several teaching and research networks were established in the year 2000. Two collaborative teaching programmes were based in South Africa at the Universities of Cape Town[5] and Pretoria[6] and one was based in Nigeria at the University of Ibadan[7]. Two research networks were established. One of them was based in Burkina Faso at the University of Ouagadougou with Fourah Bay College in Sierra Leone, Cheikh Anta Diop in Senegal as partners. The second one was based at Centre d'Etude Regional pour l'Ameliration de l'Adaptation á la Sécheresse (CERAAS) in Senegal.[8] At the same time sub-regional networks of universities such as the Inter-University Council of East Africa increased research cooperation in teaching and research.[9] The African Economic Research Consortium (AERC) continued its regional postgraduate training programmes in economics and research on Africa and the world trade system, among other things.[10]

There are more research networks that help to bring together researchers in the African region that continue to play an important role in networking. Some of these are old such as the African Association for Public Administration and Management (AAPAM) in Nairobi, the African Technology Policy Research Network (ATPS) in

---

[4] Jomo Kenyatta University in Kenya and the Ghana Institute of Management and Public Administration in Ghana, are some of the many that have established strong networking relations with other institutions in the region and abroad. This is not to mention UNISA, which is the oldest distance learning university in the world.

[5] The University of Cape Town hosted the University Science, Humanities and Engineering Partnership in Africa (USHEPIA) whose members were the University of Cape Town, and the Universities of Dar Es Salaam, Botswana, Zambia and Zimbabwe and Makerere University in Uganda and Jomo Kenyatta University in Kenya

[6] University of Pretoria hosted a Masters Degree Programme in Human Rights Law with members being the Universities of Pretoria, Botswana, Dar Es Salaam, Namibia, Zambia and Zimbabwe

[7] The University of Ibadan hosted a Masters' Degree Programme on Humanitarian and Refugee Studies with universities from Nigeria, Ghana, Burundi, Guinea, Liberia, Sudan, Sierra Leone and Mozambique as partners

[8] The Centre coordinated a graduate teaching and research programme in Microbiology for the universities of Ouagadougou, Lome (Togo), Niamey (Niger), Conakry (Guinea) and Concody (Côte d'Ivore).

[9] The IUC programmes include collaborative research on the Great Lakes, staff exchange and collaborative teaching programmes.

[10] AERC has published a good number of refereed books and journals on several key issues including the WTO system.

Nairobi, the African Centre for Technology Studies (ACTS) also based in Nairobi, the Council for Development and Social Research in Africa (CODESRIA) in Dakar and the Organisation for Social Sciences Research in Eastern Africa (OSSREA) in Addis Ababa, just to mention a few. New networks of researchers have also emerged and the number will continue to grow. They include the Southern African Regional Universities Association (SARUA), the Southern Africa Research in Management Association, (SARIMA) and the West African Research in Management Association (WARIMA) and several others.

The fifth major change is related to delivery methods. In performing their universal function of knowledge creation and dissemination and increasing access to higher education in their countries, the majority of institutions surveyed in the ADEA study have adopted new creative ways of increasing access. Apart from increased enrolments and introducing policies aimed at gender equality and regional equity (AAU 2004:66-68), they have introduced distance learning programmes and mounted institutional systems of quality assurance and enhancement (AAU 2004: 60-65). They have introduced short courses and developed institutions such as centres for external or continuing education in order to deliver courses to working people or learners in regions located far away from main campuses.[11] Sixth, lifelong learning has now been accepted as a norm in most tertiary institutions. Neglected for long in national policy agendas and development partner priorities, lifelong learning has remained for long time a strategy limited to developed countries. Lifelong learning emphasises education systems that are geared towards equipping citizens to acquire skills that enhance their employability and prepare countries for competitive participation in global knowledge driven economic systems (Torres, 2004: 86, Obanya 2004: 124).

The trends identified in the 2004 ADEA study also indicate that universities across the region are shifting from learning for the sake of it, to imparting skills that enhance employability, adaptability, creativity, competitiveness and innovation. In the study, this is shown by increasing efforts for partnership with industry, establishment of centres for technology and innovation, such as the concept of Regional Colleges of Applied Arts, Science and Technology (RECAAST)

---

[11] The University of Namibia for example has nine outreach centres for teaching and dissemination of knowledge which are used for distance learning, foundation courses to prepare admitted students with lower qualifications to undertake courses in medicine and engineering and to diffuse agricultural technology to farmers. The University of Cape Coast in Ghana has similar programmes, just to mention a few.

[12] The University of Dar Es Salaam has incorporated teaching colleges and several institutes of tertiary education into the university system while the University of Namibia has incorporated agricultural colleges into the university system and in South Africa technical colleges have been merged with universities as will be discussed shortly.

introduced in the national higher education policy in Ghana (AAU 2004: 48).[12] In other studies, it is shown by efforts to shift emphasis on the content of knowledge in terms of what is learnt and how it is capable of being transformed into technology and economic growth (Prewitt, 2004: 38-39); tailoring courses to the needs of learners rather than to the perceptions of these needs by education institutions (Obanya: 2004: 95-96); regulating quality through self-assessment and tracer studies and renewed interest in the link between higher education and lower levels of education. The Strategic Plan of the University of Namibia, for example, lists delivery of education in secondary schools as a challenge to higher education in the country and undertakes to improve it in order to improve higher education.[13]

2.2.   Organisational and Financial Reforms

In line with the general trend of reforms discussed in the ADEA study of 2004, are organisational and financial reforms covered in other studies as will be shown below. Some of organisational reforms of the past two decades include the process of *consolidation* mainly achieved through mergers. South Africa has provided what could become a long-term institutional governance reform model for the region. Through a radical programme, the South African government has used mergers to achieve multiple goals (Hall, Symes and Luecher, 2004). In trying to address inequities of the past and achieving economies of size and scale for example, it merged several HEIs and through these mergers, the tertiary education system in South Africa has managed to lay grounds for increasing social and economic integration, establishing new inclusive governance structures, redesigning systems of academic delivery and curriculum planning, setting frameworks for new and harmonised conditions of service, integrating financial management and accounting systems, streamlining cost sharing policies and developing common frameworks for the support of students and library systems (Hall, Symes and Luescher 2004: 42).

Financial instability has been an endemic feature of higher education in Africa. For a long time, it was precipitated by lack of clear formulae for funding higher education in most countries with the exception of South Africa (Pillay 2004), political tensions between universities and governments during the eighties and limited capability on the part of university leaders to counter the instability (Ekong and Swayerr 1999: 2-4; Omari and Mihyo 1991). Prominent however, were the misplaced perceptions about low rates of return on higher education in Africa, which were started by two prominent economists, Todaro and Richards in 1972 at a

---

Strategic Objective 4 of the *Third Five Strategic Plan 2006-2010 of the University of Namibia,* University of Namibia, Windhoek, p. 37.

donor conference in Bellagio Italy, to which African scholars were never invited and which dominated thinking about and support for higher education for three decades[14], though strongly and constantly resisted by some donor agencies such Sida, UNESCO, UNICEF and UNDP (Torres 2004:55-76) and refuted by reputed scholars in and outside Africa (Ekong and Sawyerr, 1999: 4; Teal, 2001, Appelton, 2001, Sawyerr, 2002).

In the last two decades, African higher education institutions have taken constructive measures to stem the tide of financial instability. They have introduced cost sharing through fees and student loan systems, but the impact of these measures has not been uniformly positive. In some cases, lack of systems to support loans has reduced the possibilities of increasing equitable access to higher education, which many tertiary institutions on the continent hold out as a core value (Woodhall, 2004: 43-45, Johnstone 2004: 22-23, Ishengoma, 2004:112-114). However, in some countries such as Kenya and Uganda, while these policies have increased the equity gap, proper cost-recovery systems have enabled governments to build a reliable base for financing higher education through student loans (Musisi and Muwanga, 1993:35-6, Mayanja 2005:228, Otieno, 2004:84-87).

Academic entrepreneurship, a term used by Barnett (2000:409) and Clark (1998, 2004), has also been attempted through the design of short courses with lower delivery costs and high returns, the establishment of public service training centres and business schools,[15] the launch of hands-on, demand-driven business management programmes with the support of commercial and financial institutions[16]; the establishment of research and consultancy bureaus, specialised production units, general production and services units as in the case of universities in Kenya (Kiamba, 2004: 62-63) and externally funded outreach programmes such as those of KIST in Rwanda (Butare, 2004:44-50) just to mention a few. Additional methods of financing higher education such as increasing the number of R&D commercial institutions following the example of the University of Lagos, or increasing links with the productive sectors as has been attempted at the Obafemi Awolowo University at Ile Ife (Aina 2003: 20-23), and maximum utilisation of land

---

[14] Their paper at the Bellagio conference on 'Education and Development Reconsidered' titled 'Educational Demand and Supply in the Context of Growing Unemployment in Less Developed Nations' is analyzed by Carl K. Escher in 'African Universities: Overcoming Intellectual Dependency' in T.M Yesufu (Ed.), 1973 *Creating the African University. Emerging Issues of the 1970s*. Oxford University Press, Ibadan.

[15] The University of Namibia Centre for Public Service Training for example runs senior public managers' courses. The University of Witwatersrand Business School, has been recently accepted as a model of how to run a profitable and yet high quality business school in the region.

[16] As in the case of the Jomo Kenyatta University of Agriculture Science and Technology, the University of Ghana Business School and the Ghana Institute of Management and Public Administration just to mention a few outstanding examples.

and accommodation potential on commercial basis as has been attempted by some universities in Kenya, (Abagi 2003:181-3) could strengthen the entrepreneurship drive in higher education institutions.

All these organisational, governance, financial and curriculum reforms and measures have created a base for strategic management in tertiary education institutions in Africa. They have put in place the necessary conditions for the establishment of learning systems that can promote lifelong learning, relevance of academic programmes, linkages between tertiary and other levels of education and the necessary policy frameworks for cooperative competition and competitive cooperation between institutions of tertiary education at national and regional levels. Although the impact of these reforms on the relevance of curricula and financial stability in higher education institutions is yet to be properly assessed, there are indications that they are having a positive effect. The first indicator is the increasing number of paying students at undergraduate and postgraduate levels across the region. The numbers are overwhelming, which indicate that the rush for courses abroad is decreasing and customer confidence is increasing. Secondly and related to this, HEIs in the region have initiated second stream financial sources through evening courses and extra-mural services. These, though increasing the stress and strain on restricted staffing capacity as we shall see below, are indicators that demand for services is increasing, relevance is being acknowledged by the various stakeholders and HEIs are not in the same type of financial crises they experienced in the eighties.

The primary obstacle to the achievement of these and other reform and innovation goals; however, is staff capacity erosion. Before, during and after the reforms, capacity erosion through brain drain and general staff turnover has remained a significant setback to the human resources stability and the strategic readiness of tertiary institutions to use these reforms to deliver on their missions and visions and make further strides into the global knowledge society. In the next section, the dimensions of these problems are examined.

3.0. Staff Capacity Erosion as a Threat to Innovative Reforms: Systemic Issues

In organisational capacity development, there are six key areas that need to be given utmost attention. The first and perhaps most important area is human resources mainly staff numbers and relevant competencies, recruitment and retention procedures and strategies, staff development, training and advancement, performance appraisal and preparation for exit. The second key area is infrastructure and technology. For academic institutions, this includes classrooms, offices, hostels, laboratories, libraries, resource centres, computer facilities, online resources, equipment, chemicals and transport facilities. The third area is that of financial resources in terms of subventions, grants, donations, revenues, reserves, endowments and loans. The fourth area is that of strategic leadership and management revolving around governance and decision-making, participation, corporate culture, incentive structures, performance management systems, inputs, outputs and outcomes management and measurement and labour management practices. The fifth area is the structure of programme management characterised by programme planning, monitoring and evaluation, reporting, accountability and communication systems. The sixth area is networking and links with key stakeholders such as research and teaching networks, other HEIs, alumni, sponsors, donors and similar stakeholders, customers, partners and private service providers.[17]

The most critical element for all; however, is the human resources factor. Without strengthening human resources and retaining the critical skills and competencies within any organisation, other components stand to suffer. In academic institutions, the critical human capital includes academic, administrative and technical staff resources. The institutional, governance, management and financial reforms undertaken as seen above will be more sustainable if there is stability in the area of human resources. Unfortunately, several factors still militate against this stability. Although staff turnover is decreasing in certain faculties such as the humanities, there is still acute shortage of staff in faculties such as agriculture, natural resources, engineering, medicine, management and law. This was the case in six of the seven HEIs covered by this study. The only exception was the Ghana Institute of Management and Public Administration, which is specialising in management and law. In all the rest, there is also shortage of academic and technical staff in IT departments, while in the sciences there is an increased shortage of technical staff. It seems the improvement in the economies of countries such as Ghana, Rwanda and Zambia is creating opportunity for technical staff to drift from academic institutions to the private and other sectors. While the general definition of brain drain for the purposes of this study has been confined to mobility of staff from developing to developed countries, as we shall see below, for organisations losing staff, be they HEIs or others, it does not so much matter where such staff is drifting to. What matters is the gap created by such a drift. In this section, we will examine general trends in capacity erosion through brain drain and migration of highly qualified experts from African higher education institutions to developed countries, and institutional and capacity problems related to policy formulation and management that aggravate this problem at regional and national levels.

---

[17] Based on core operational and adaptive capacities in research organisations used by Douglas Horton et al, 2003, *Evaluating Capacity Development. Experiences from Research and Development Organisations Around the World*, ISNAR, CTA, IDRC, p.28

3.1. Brain Drain, Brain Exchange and Brain Gain

Brain drain has been defined as, 'the permanent or long-term international emigration of skilled people who have been the subject of considerable educational investment by their own societies' (Wickramasekara 2002: 3). Other definitions confine themselves to the migration of highly skilled professionals to other countries irrespective of investments in the education of such professionals by their countries (Findlay 2002:4). Some scholars however, prefer to use the term 'scientific mobility' (Logue 2007:75) because they argue that the concept of brain drain is heavily loaded with nationalistic values, which should not apply in the era of globalisation. In the context of higher education in Africa, brain drain has been described as a process through which a significant number of academic staff is lost to other sectors within the country or to other countries (Ishengoma 2007, Yaqub 2007:24). While all definitions have their own appeal and justification, scientific mobility and brain drain are not the same. Some protagonists tend even to argue that the concept of brain drain denies the right of developing countries to participate in the international brain exchange and argue that migration of skilled professionals should be seen as positive. Without denying that brain drain leads to exposure and acquisition of knowledge, technology and skills that become useful to sending countries in case the migrants return, there is a tendency to treat brain drain, brain exchange and brain gain as if they are synonymous. The three concepts mean different things and need not be used as if they are interchangeable.

Brain drain is essentially a transfer of human resources that creates a structural human resource gap in the source country. All countries have experienced brain drain at any time in their history. Some developed countries still experience brain drain and all developed countries are engaged in a struggle to attract talent and if possible reduce the migration of their skilled professionals to other countries. Canada, for example, has a serious problem of losing professionals to the US. The United Kingdom was for quite some time suffering from brain drain of its professionals to the US, Australia, New Zealand and Europe. But most of the developed countries no longer experience brain drain. They have managed to attract professionals from other countries, while losing some of their own. Some have reached a stage where they lose some and get professionals from other countries to fill the gap. When a country has reached such a stage, it is no longer experiencing brain drain, but it is engaged in brain exchange. When it manages to gain more than it loses, it graduates from brain exchange to brain gain. Hence, a country that is a net exporter of skilled professionals and therefore a net loser, cannot speak of brain exchange or brain gain. A country that does not have a net surplus of skilled personnel in that it gains more than it loses on the international labour market is engaged in brain exchange, but cannot talk of brain gain. Brain gain is a situation where a country attracts more professionals from other countries than it loses to them or gets its own professionals to return in such high numbers that the inflows become higher than the outflows. This is what makes African countries different from those of Europe or North America and even some of the East Asian countries.

As has been pointed out by many researchers, Africa is the worst hit of all continents by brain drain. According to Wackramasekara (2002:5) between 1985 and 1990, the continent lost 60,000 professionals mainly doctors, engineers and university lecturers; 60% of all Ghanaian doctors trained locally in the 1980s had left the country by the year 2000, while in Sudan, 17% of doctors, 20% of lecturers and 30% of the engineers left in one year alone (1978). The International Organisation for Migration (IOM) had estimated that by the year 2000, about 300,000 professionals of African origins were working in Europe and North America (Cervantes and Sueller 2005). According to Mazrui, the most highly educated ethnic group in the US as indicated by the US Census Bureau, is the population of Nigerians living in that country! (Yaqub 2007: 23). Figures cited by (Marfouk 2007: 99) indicate that by 2000 Cape Verde had lost 67% of its professionals to OECD countries, the Gambia 63%, the Seychelles[18] 59%, Sierra Leone 53% and Mozambique 45%. With one of the highest per capita incomes in the developing world, the fact that the Seychelles has lost more people than conflict countries such as Sierra Leone is very disturbing. In such a situation, it may be consoling but very misleading for any African scholars to talk about brain exchange in the context of the African continent. Africa remains a net exporter of skilled labour to other countries and higher education institutions in addition to the health and other education sub-sectors remain the most affected.

A 1993 World Bank study of seven African universities[19] on the problems relating to retention in African universities (Blair and Jordan 1994) established that although the numbers of expatriate teaching staff had declined in African universities due to the increase in numbers of national graduates, the overall budget for education had dropped from 16.6 % of government budgets in 1980 to 15.2 % in 1990. The share of higher education budgets had decreased from an average of 19.1% in 1980-84 to 17. 6% in 1985-88. It was estimated in this study that 23, 000 academics were leaving the continent every year and over 10,000 of highly qualified Nigerians were employed in the US alone at that time. On the causes of the exodus, the study identified low salaries and conflicts between students and governments in general, but noted that staff retention problems were also compounded by 'weak institutional management capacity in the area of personnel' characterised by absence of job descriptions, weak accountability systems, poor monitoring mechanisms and poor capacity utilisation.

---

[18] The Seychelles has one of the highest per capita incomes in the world, higher than some of the Southern European countries.
[19] National University of Benin, University of Botswana, University of Ghana, University of Ibadan, Makerere University, University of Zambia and University of Zimbabwe.

The above study noted however, that apart from the University of Zambia, appropriate staff numbers had been maintained in the other universities it covered, staff student ratios were manageable, over half of existing staff expressed willingness to continue working for their universities, most staff valued the autonomy they enjoyed in the way they organised their work and the majority of those who had left expressed readiness to return if conditions of employment were improved. Ten years later, the World Bank sponsored another study of the same universities to which was added the University of KwaZulu-Natal (Tettey, 2006). At that time, most things had changed. Some of the reforms covered in the previous section were beginning to take place and state control of academic institutions was beginning to be relaxed, although funding levels for higher education had not improved. This helped the researcher to focus more on the management issues raised in the Blair and Jordan study. From these two studies and others related to the issue of staff losses in higher education institutions, it is emerging that there are systemic issues at regional and national levels that tend to encourage the continued drain of African brains to other economies. In the next sub-section some of these issues are examined.

3.2. Systemic issues at regional and national levels that encourage brain drain in Higher Education Institutions (HEIs)

Systemic issues relate to the way regional bodies and national authorities organise themselves to respond to the challenges of the international labour market. The systems in question relate to policy formulation, implementation, monitoring, review and innovation mechanisms and most importantly, the policies themselves. In the present study and that one carried out by Tettey and corroborated by others as will be shown in the discussion, it is clear that there are two types of obstacles to retention of staff in African institutions of tertiary education. The first set is that of systemic issues in the relationship between governments themselves in the region and these governments and their national institutions of tertiary education. The second set relates to management systems within these institutions themselves. The latter will be covered in section 4.

3.2.1. The policy framework

The policy formulation and management framework at regional and national level is very weak. In the context of brain drain, this reflects both the impact of the drain on African institutions and the fact that the structural weaknesses caused by this drain continue to affect the capacity of regional bodies and national authorities to adequately assess the consequences of the drain and redress them. At the moment, some countries in Europe and North America and a few countries in Asia are experiencing shifts from brain exchange to brain gain. The net inflow of experienced and highly skilled workers is higher than the outflow. In the UK, the change has been rapid since the 1990s. Between 1992 and 1998, there was dramatic increase of migrants from English speaking countries to the UK as the latter transformed itself from a garrisoned or fortress economy to an open economy for skilled professionals. During this period, Britain managed to get a surplus of 136, 700 skilled workers comparing inflows and outflows (Findlay 2002: 4) The UK managed to attain this position by adopting four strategic policies that helped it to reverse the trend from brain exchange to brain gain. First and foremost, it encouraged the inflow of the so-called 'transient migrants' (Findlay 2002: 11). These are migrants who are highly skilled coming for short periods and returning to their countries or moving to other countries. This group was targeted through UK multinationals operating abroad as they were encouraged to bring into the country highly skilled professionals for short periods. This enabled the multinationals not only to fill the skills gaps, but also to learn from and acquire knowledge and experience from foreign experts.

Second, in 2000 the British government launched a £20 million project aimed at supporting British engineers and technologists working abroad to come back home. This project aimed at compensating and repatriating such experts, seems to have worked very well (Cervantes and Sueller 2005).Third, in the year 2000 the UK government introduced new immigration regulations that removed restrictions on work permits for highly skilled experts and their spouses, relaxed visa requirements for students and made it easier for such students to get extension of visas and those on long programmes and their spouses to work and stay longer in the country after graduation. This was one of the most beneficial policies for the UK, because after the new immigration regulations were passed, applications and approvals for work permits increased by 70% within one year. Immediately after the new regulations were launched, out of the 16 countries with the highest number of work permits, South Africa came sixth, Nigeria tenth and Zimbabwe thirteenth!! (Findley 2002: 12).

In the case of South Africa, another UK policy increased its vulnerability to brain drain by encouraging South African citizens to hold double passports. Findley (2002) estimated that by the year 2000, about 800,000 South Africans were holding British passports. The fourth strategy was aimed at reducing the dependency of the UK economy on foreign workers. To counter this trend in the long run, it has launched training programmes and increased funding for training for the IT sectors. The UK is not the only country that has adopted such strategies to shift from brain exchange to net brain gain. Canada, Germany and the US operate a green card system and Australia and New Zealand have for a long time operated skill-based immigration policies. The number of foreign born Nobel Prize winners in the UK and US testifies to the scientific gains these countries have made beyond numbers and the highest number of publications on Africa associated with American, Canadian and European universities are by scholars of African origin.[20]

While the European Union and other developed regions have spent the last two decades removing legal and other obstacles to the migration of highly qualified experts to their economies (Schmid 2007), countries in Africa do not have the necessary organisational structures and frameworks for developing policies to retain their scarce human resources[21]. Some of the policies that have remained operational in several countries in Africa actually promote negative factors that compel people to leave the continent. Migration laws do not make it easy for experts to circulate within the region. Xenophobia in some countries is higher than in some countries in the North. It is easier for African experts to migrate to OECD countries than to move within the region even for short visits. The biggest constraint, however has been in the area of policy implementation at regional and national levels.

Between 1980 and the year 2000, the UN Economic Commission for Africa (ECA) and the African Union invested substantial resources and efforts in the development of policies and policy frameworks for enhancing the contribution of education, generally, and higher education, in particular, to social and economic change in Africa. Although the UNDP Human Development Report of 1996 recorded the 1980s as a 'lost decade' for Africa, African leaders did not give up on chances for Africa's recovery. Beginning in the early 1990s together with their global partners, they began looking for new avenues through which to salvage the African economies. Following the launch of the UN Programme of Action for Africa's Economic Recovery and Development 1986-90 (UN-PAAARD), the ECA and the OAU (now AU), launched several home-grown initiatives aimed at reversing Africa's processes of decline, which were causing the continent to lose its best resources including human capital.

In the OAU Resolution on International Cooperation for African Economic and Social Recovery and Development, the African Heads of State and Government acknowledged the role of international financial institutions and donor agencies in supporting Africa's recovery, but called upon them to strengthen local initiatives and reduce the burden of debt on the poor countries.[22] In March 1991, the African Leadership Forum led by General Olusegun Obasanjo (former President of Nigeria) managed to get prominent world leaders to Helsinki for the 'International

---

[20] For example the first African to be honoured by the University of Copenhagen as the best scholar recently is Professor Mohamed Salih a Sudanese prolific writer based at the Unversity of Leiden who published 21 books on Africa between 1995 and 2005 in addition to other numerous publications.

21 The Bologna and Barcelona processes provide European countries and their universities a platform and framework to develop common positions on how to protect themselves from adverse effects of competition for skills and how to use higher education as a tool for competition. See for example the decisions on the implications of GATS for higher education on http://www.unige.ch/eua/Eng/activities/wto.

Roundtable on a Conference on Security, Stability, Development and Cooperation in Africa. The same year several other important policies were designed by the African leaders and launched. Together, they indicated their determination to prepare Africa for dynamic participation in the global economy in the new millennium[23].

While all these initiatives created a number of tasks to be performed if development had to be achieved, the issue of critical competences and skills necessary to carry them through remained pivotal to all measures and activities. In a coordinated series of meetings of ministers responsible for human resources development the ECA and OAU (as it then was) launched a concerted effort to design and launch policies and programmes on human resources development. Meeting in Khartoum earlier in 1988, the African Heads of State and Government passed what came to be known as the 'Khartoum Declaration on Human Resources for Socio-economic Recovery and Development.' As a follow up to this declaration, the ECA organised several meetings of ministers of human resources development to formulate policies that could be used to implement it.

The major policy outcome of that initiative was the 'Africa's Human Resources Agenda for the 1990s and Beyond' passed in November 1991. The timing of this agenda was crucial. Human resources were pivotal to the success of all other programmes. The Agenda was a comprehensive document aimed at supporting all other programmes including the 'UN Programme of Action for Africa's Economic Recovery and Development' (UN-PAARD) which was later replaced by the UN New Agenda for the Development of Africa' launched in September 1991 and other international programmes aimed at Africa's recovery.[24]

The main pillars of the human resources development agenda were:
-    Strengthening education as a means of laying grounds for self-reliance;
-    Building capacity for effective management;
-    Improving human resources support for policy formulation;

---

[22] Resolution 196 (XXVI) Preamble and Clauses 2,3&4

[23] Some of the key policies include The Kampala Document Towards A Conference on Security, Stability, Development and Cooperation in Africa May 1991; The OAU Resolution on The Global Coalition for Africa, Resolution 203 (XXVII) 3-5 June, 1991; the Abidjan Declaration on Debt Relief, Recovery and Democracy in Africa, July 1991 and the Abuja Treaty establishing the African Economic Community, June 1991.

[24] International commitments to the process were expressed through the Speech by the President of the World Bank, Barber Conable titled, 'Africa's Development and Destiny' at the 27th Session of the OAU Assembly of Heads of State and Government, 3 June 1991; a statement by the North-South Roundtable titled, 'Towards a 'Development Contract', delivered by Arve Ostad, Arne Tostensen and Tom Vraalsen of Michelsen Institute of Norway, in Ottawa, June 1991; and the UN New Agenda for the Development of Africa in the 1990s' New York, September 14, 1991.

- Reducing unemployment especially among graduates of institutions of higher learning;
- Making higher education relevant to the needs of African economies;
- Facilitating the capability of higher education to establish internal engines of growth;
- Supporting higher education to train people for entrepreneurship, excellence in management, environmental protection and the reduction of dependency; and
- Supporting higher education to provide skills for production.[25]

The policy also addressed issues of unemployment. The 27th Session of the Assembly of Heads of State and Government passed a declaration on, "The Employment Crisis in Africa,"[26] followed by several other policy documents on the employment crisis that was linked to education and human resources.[27] The link between education and employment was given a lot of emphasis and in order to enable institutions of higher learning to help in the increase of socio-economic growth and reduction of unemployment, it was recommended that governments had to revitalise institutions of higher learning by:
- Increasing resources for them to enable them to teach, conduct research and provide services to their communities;
- Increasing the relevance of higher education by developing curricula and changing the course offerings in favour of sciences;
- Increasing access to higher education after noting that in 1987 only 2% of the total enrolment in the education systems in Africa was in higher education;
- Restoring the morale of the teaching force in higher education through working conditions, monetary incentives and funding for research; and
- Establishing a regional framework for regional cooperation in higher education to allow resource sharing.

By all standards, the proposed measures reflected a deep understanding of the problem facing higher education institutions and if implemented they stood a chance for revitalising institutions of higher learning.

Apart from these special conferences devoted to human resources, higher education and development, between 1990 and 2000, there were 19 world conferences on education generally and six regional conferences on education in the African

---

[25] ECA, 1991, *Africa's Human Resources Agenda for the 1990s and Beyond*, ECA Document No. E/ECA/PHSD/MC/91/6(6.3)(ii)(a).
[26] See E/ECA/PHSD/TC/WP.6
[27] Refer to the 'African Employment Challenge for the 1990s' Document No. E/ECA/PHSD/TC/91/CRP.2 and the policy on "Strategies for Manpower Utilization and the Unemployment Crisis in Africa' In Document No. E/ECA/PHSD/TC/91/CRP.1 (6.2iii)

region.[28] Of all policy documents however, it was the human resources agenda that covered issues touching on high level skills and technical and technological capabilities. The agenda had sought to use education to tackle the problems of unemployment, stagnation or retrogression and excessive dependency on external inputs, knowledge and other resources.

In spite of the clarity of the policy documents, the failure of many governments to extend to institutions of higher learning the support they deserved seems to have reduced the impact of the human resources agenda and consequently all other policies whose success depended on the agenda. It should be acknowledged; however, that apart from neglect, failure to transform education in Africa has other historical and operational explanations, such as lack of link with national development goals; constant changes in curriculum without linking changes to needs; dependency on project funding and the failure to build education into structures of local culture and languages and other factors.[29]

Like several regional policies before it, the human resources agenda was very detailed and reflected a determination on the part of the African governments to strengthen higher education institutions, and use them as a springboard for a sustained development initiative. But in spite of the depth and breadth of its provisions, the policy does not seem to have had a lot of impact on the ground. The situation as reflected throughout the 1990s does not show that the human resources agenda was even given a chance for success. On the contrary, the institutions of higher learning were in bad shape and while the 1990 UNDP Human Development Report had estimated that 100 million people in Africa were unemployed, at the end of the 1990s the number seemed to have gone up by 20% with underemployment in rural areas rising even higher.

Graduate unemployment that the agenda sought to reduce had increased and Africa lost a lot of trained experts to other economies. According to N. Ndiaye, the Deputy Director of the International Migration Organisation in Geneva, between 1995 and 2000, Congo (DRC) alone lost more than 1.7 million people through migration abroad, while estimates for countries such as Burkina Faso, Burundi, Guinea, Mali, Sudan and Tanzania, the average was more than 200,000 people per country during the same period. (IOM, 2001:27). In 1992, the proportion of African professional

---

[28] These include the 1991 Dakar Sixth Conference of Ministers of Education and those Responsible for Economic Planning in African Member States (MINEDAF); the 1993 Ouagadougou Conference on Education for Girls; Audience Africa 1995, the Kampala Conference on the Empowerment of Women through Functional Literacy and the Education of the Girl-Child, 1996, MINEDAF VII in Durban 1998 and the 1999 OUA Conference of African Ministers of Education: COMEDAF in Harare.
[29] See some of the reasons are adduced by Prof. Pai Obanya in Obanya, P., 2002, *Revitalising Education in Africa*, Stirling - Horden Publishers (Ng) Ltd, Lagos, pp. 22-23

workers as a proportion of all foreign workers in the United Kingdom was 23.1%. In 1999, it was already 31.9% (Findlay 2002: 48).

Enrolment in higher learning institutions increased slightly due to increase in the number of universities, but the increase was not phenomenal. At a lower level, it had been expected that enrolment for children of school going age would have gone up between 1990 and the year 2000. But figures for 1998 showed that the percentage of children not going to school at all had risen in many countries reaching the alarming rate of 70-80% in Guinea Bissau and Madagascar; 60-70% in Angola, Malawi and Mozambique; 50-60% in Togo and Chad and 20-40% in the majority of the remaining countries. Only in Djibouti, Nigeria, Senegal and Sudan were the figures below 10%.[30] In addition, the Human Development Report for 1997 observed that income poverty had increased in Africa, the incidence of poverty having gone up to 42% and that of income poverty to 38%[31].

These developments raise very important issues about the interface between policy formulation and policy implementation at regional level. The next sub-section seeks to identify what makes it possible or difficult for policies to become implemented at regional level. The assumption is that the human resource agenda was the pivotal policy that could have enabled other policies including those of donors and international agencies to be implemented, and the failure of that policy to be implemented as planned may have influenced the success or failure to implement the other policies. It hypothesised here that if the agenda had been successfully implemented, economic growth would have tremendously increased and Africa would have graduated from brain drain to brain exchange. But caught up in an egg and chicken situation, capacity deficits were caused by among other things, brain drain and due to that, African countries could not and still face problems of development that prevent them from formulating and implementing policies that could lift them out of the brain drain trap.

3.2.2. Policy Implementation Capacity Deficits

African leaders have been accused of talking too much and doing too little. But this ignores the policy management capacity deficits they experience. Some of these deficits are due to capacity erosion that brain drain has caused over a long period of time forcing most of them to operate with acutely understaffed establishments in spite of ever increasing national and international obligations. The main symptom of policy management failure lies in the incapacity of many governments to translate international resolutions into national policies or where they are enacted, to turn

---

[30] *World Education Review*, 1998
[31] UNDP, *Human Development Report* 1997, UNDP, NY, p.47

them into policies and the failure to effectively implement them. As mentioned earlier, between 1990 and 2000, 19 world conferences were held on education and attended by African leaders.[32] On the African continent alone, six conferences were organised on education. Why for example, do leaders find it easier to make commitments at regional level and more difficult to implement them at national level? Within existing discourses about factors that influence decisions about policymaking, we may begin to consider some basic factors. First, is the key issue of efficiency.

Efficiency is used as a subjective factor that is determinant of policy action. When, for example, a policy maker is confronted with the choice of whether to use the limited number of drafting personnel to take up the issue of privatisation or competition policy under pressure from donor agencies or to use them to pass a new education bill, the choice is clear. The limited resources will be used for those activities carrying a penalty, if not carried out. Discussing the major factors policy makers take into account in policy formulation, Vassant Moharir (2003:113) outlines six: efficiency, effectiveness, responsiveness, innovation, political feasibility and administrative feasibility. Using these factors to examine the interface between regional policy formulation and local policy implementation, one can assume that given the limited number of human and financial resources, many leaders will find it easy to make commitments abroad, but they may consider it inefficient to devote those limited resources to external commitments if there are no internal or external pressures for their implementation. It is also logical that the criterion of effectiveness when used, implies that the policy makers will easily choose policies they find easy to implement given the capacity contexts they are operating in. In the absence of local knowledge about commitments made abroad or pressures from within for implementation of such commitments, if the achievement of the goals seems more distant and less certain, they will choose to postpone them and implement those they find easier to implement.

Responsiveness is important as regards the demand orientation of a policy objective. If the demand emanates from outside and is not accompanied by any pressure of sanction or loss of face or votes locally, there is a possibility that policy commitments made abroad will be shelved in favour of local policies whose demand emanates from within the country. Hence, no matter how legitimate a policy objective may be, its demand orientation may determine the responsiveness of the state to it. The criterion of innovation is also influential. In many situations, the politicians adopt a cost-and-benefit approach to innovation. Innovations in higher education may have

---

[32] These include MINEDAF VI and VII held in Dakar 1991 and Durban 1998, two conferences on the education of girls one in Ouagadougou 1993 and another in Kampala 1996, Audience Africa in Paris 1995 and COMEDAF in Harare 1999.

long-term benefits, but these benefits may not be obvious to the public and may not be vote winners except among those who realize their value. In addition, because institutions of higher learning are normally removed from the communities, the public rarely notices their decline. Even as they decline, they still look like ivory towers compared to their surrounding environments. Hence even their physical rehabilitation let alone their total revitalisation may not be easily appreciated by the majority of the people.

This adds strength to Moharir's fourth criteria of political feasibility. Although by this, Moharir refers mainly to acceptability by key sectors in the economy or bureaucrats etc., it can also be explained in the light of cost-benefit analysis. If by building roads the policy makers will be seen to be committed to increasing transport facilities for people and goods, they will give transport priority over higher education. Similarly where the relations between government and HEI leaders are not close due to political or historical factors, administratively, higher education may become a less feasible option than other services. In addition, to reward supporters and win new ones, policy makers can use policy choices in circumstances of limited resources. It can also be used to punish opponents especially where students in HEIs are seen as allies of the political opposition. Hence, policymaking can become a form of patronage.[33] Higher education institutions tend to be difficult to patronise and this creates difficulties for them.

If we go beyond these six criteria, we can also accept the fact that policymaking requires capacity. Those who take capacity for policymaking and the linear model of policymaking as granted, believe implementation follows automatically from formulation. According to Thomas and Grindle, for example, 'Successful implementation is viewed as a question of whether or not the implementing institution is strong enough for the task. If implementation is unsuccessful, the usual remedy is to call for greater efforts to strengthen institutional capacity or to blame failure on lack of political will...'[34] But in actual practice, implementation reveals that to get the things done involves a multitude of actors with various motives and capabilities, who also interact with one another. Those actors and the factors that influence their perceptions and capabilities will always shape the nature of the policymaking. For many African countries, especially those that were severely hit by the economic crises of the seventies and eighties, such capacity does not exist and brain drain has had its share in its erosion.

---

[33] Manzetti, **L.**, (1993), *"The Political Economy of Privatization Through Divestiture in Lesser Developed Economies"*, in *Comparative Politics*, Vol. 25, pp. 429-453.
: 17).
[34] **Grindle, M.S and John W. Thomas, (1991),** 'Implementing Reforms: Arenas, Stakes and Resources' in *Public Choices and Public Changes*. John Hopkins University Press. P.122.

Finally, to carry out policy formulation, there is a need for core competencies within government departments. Such capabilities involve analytical capabilities, administrative capacity, networking capabilities, networking skills, leadership, evaluation mechanisms, communication infrastructure and most importantly, human and information mobility. A cohesive team of experts is required and it has to have hands-on experience of the formulation process, knowledge of the local situation and information about resources required and their sources. Such capacity has been lacking for a long time and brain drain has been part of the causes for capacity deficits in the policy management area. As a result, African governments have been unable to address the problem in a systematic and coordinated way. Suggestions on how to improve the policy framework, such as the formation of an African Higher Education Area (Mihyo 2004:136-7), and the strengthening of the regional mechanisms for policy making on higher education under the Arusha Convention (Shabani, 2004), have been made at various fora. Unless such capacity gaps are filled, there will continue to be a gap between regional and international commitments on the one hand, and national policies, on the other.

3.2.3. Funding formulae and statistics

One major disadvantage for African countries is the *wage gap between* them and developed nations. Though Blair and Jordan (1994) on the one hand, and Tettey (2006), on the other, did not go deeply into this problem, Ndulu (2004: 69- 70) has raised the real wage advantage of developed countries over developing countries. He addresses the problem together with the demographic factors that create demand for foreign skills in recipient countries and create big numbers of skilled youths that cannot be absorbed or adequately paid when absorbed on the labour market in African countries. He concludes that with these two factors continuing to play a role in the labour market relations between developed and African countries, the pressure to migrate will always persist. Shah (2007:65) has argued that sending countries cannot match the wages paid by receiving countries, although they have an international obligation to pay decent wages to their employees within their various sectors, which they fail to do forcing experts to leave.

This raises the question why higher education institutions in Africa, generally with the exception of those in the Northern and Southern regions, with all the skills they control and while their staff teach students and communities how to develop businesses and create wealth, they cannot mobilise these skills to generate enough resources to pay their staff decent wages and retain them. Three factors are important when it comes to this question. The first one is how the activities of HEIs in Africa are evaluated and funded. In the majority of cases, the funding formula for HEIs is arbitrary. The governments undertake to pay for salaries, students, institutional support and infrastructure. These are administratively determined and adjusted at will by the governments without consultation, justification or accountability. The core problem is the absence of a funding formula that quantifies the actual needs and attaches norms to the items that have to be funded[35].

Second, is the issue of statistics, data and information on higher education. Affecting capacity to plan effectively, allocating resources efficiently and even developing appropriate policies or funding formulae have to do with the management of data. It has an institutional and national perspective. While some progress has been made with computerisation, there are still serious data management constraints in many HIEs and education ministries, directorates and councils. Some members of staff interviewed during this study indicated that their universities did not keep proper records on them. Information on academic staff tends to be in more than one place and very few universities have a proper information policy. Assessing the crisis of data development and management at the Makerere University for example, Nakabo-Ssewanyana (1999, 2003), has expressed concern that even staff employed to manage information systems lack the necessary capacity and orientation for keeping all the necessary information on staff.

Absence of proper systems of data development and management systems can easily lead to loss of information on staff causing career stagnation and decline in job satisfaction. At national level, directorates and councils of higher education are even less organised to collect data on tertiary education bodies relating to performance, students and staff profiles, because these can only come from the institutions themselves. Where some data are available, they tend to be underutilised (Ssewanyana 1999:271-2). Lack of proper data management systems at national level is affecting the levels of support governments can extend to HEIs. In some countries, government departments in charge of higher education tend to know very little about tertiary education institutions.[36]

Therefore issues of statistics and information on higher education have more fundamental problems that affect planning, funding, proper monitoring, evaluation and accountability. Generally, the language of 'statistics' as a management tool in most HEIs is unknown. 'Statistics' is still treated as a subject taught by relevant departments in these institutions, but there are very few efforts made to make it a

---

[35] In the absence of norms in terms of student hours per course, minimum and maximum hours of teaching per week, compensation and funding for hours spent on research and outreach etc, the necessary number of full time employment (FTE) slots and the number of administrative staff slots required to carry these functions cannot be established. As a result HEIs get under-funded.

[36] In a recent allocation of financial resources to all institutions of education, a ministry of education in one African country allocated a miniscule amount for infrastructure to tertiary institutions. When asked why, the official concerned said he/she did not know the needs of these institutions because the ministry works more closely with basic education institutions than with tertiary one. This shows how important it is for universities to develop their own information and data systems and make them available to governments.

planning and management tool for accountability, efficiency and competition. Where some data are collected, they are not appropriately disaggregated on gender, regional or other relevant social basis. In the collection of data and information, relevant communities and groups including staff, students and funding agencies are not properly involved. At national level, government ministries and directorates of higher education do not seem to keep regular contacts with HIEs on data and statistics.

If planning and allocation of resources within the higher education sectors have to improve, there is a need for higher education institutions at all levels to take a new approach to data and statistics. They have to be seen as tools for improving governance and supporting allocation of resources to teaching, research and community development support. Without proper data and statistics at national level, decision making is likely to be flawed, resource allocation to remain arbitrary in most countries and conclusions on HEIs to be biased or based on speculation and conjecture. At the same time HEIs have to build statistical capacity not only for the proper management of their core functions, but also to enable them to negotiate. They need to establish strong statistical capacity to help them to:
- Track staff performance to ensure that workloads are equitably distributed between individuals and across faculties;
- Determine the actual time spent on each of their core activities and use the results in negotiations for funding or external support;
- Monitor student – staff ratios and ensure that they are balanced between faculties and at the same time, use the results to develop appropriate norms for allocation of resources across faculties and in negotiations for funding;
- Track gender balance within and across faculties and design interventions necessary to ensure a healthy and respectable gender balance;
- Develop higher education specific statistical norms and concepts on inputs, outputs and outcomes that can support strategic planning and measurement of results;
- Use data to support performance management, staff development and leadership succession;
- Form basis for information and resource sharing, leveraging and other forms of cooperation between HEIs themselves and their partners; and
- Generally, support advocacy, lobbying and fundraising activities.

Last and perhaps also important is the issue of accountability. Subject to further research, it is opined here that many departments, faculties and centres in the majority of HIEs earn substantial amounts of money from consultancy and research activities. More often than not, these funds are separately managed and in some cases they rarely feature in the accounts and financial reports of the institutions. At one of the universities visited the foreign students' short term programme was earning an average of US $3 million a year. Given the size of the institute involved, that was enough money to pay staff decent wages for a whole year and even meet other costs. At another university visited, a faculty was raising enough money out of outreach activities, which if properly accounted for and managed, is enough to pay staff wages for a whole year and even foot costs of the library. But in both cases, the funds were not accounted for in the budgets and annual reports. This may be common in other higher education institutions and in the absence of proper systems of accountability, abuse of such funds is possible and can undermine the financial base of the institutions involved and their credibility in the eyes of the public and their partners. Improved systems of accounting, accountability and institutional integrity could also help to reduce the financial problems of HEIs.

3.2.4. The regulatory framework

Another systemic problem at national level is that of unregulated and uncoordinated competition among public higher education institutions, which is partly responsible for staffing instability in some countries. Such competition between two public universities in Zambia has caused some difficulties within the same group of public institutions. For a long time the University of Zambia (UNZA) was the only public university in Zambia. After 1992 when the Copperbelt University was established, staff began to leave UNZA to join the Copperbelt University. The salaries at the Copperbelt University were higher than at UNZA, and the incentives at the former are still better than at the latter. Houses at UNZA have been sold, because they were too old but the Copperbelt University still offers housing to staff. The government has retained the same funding formula for the two universities when it is clear that the two are not at the same level in terms of size, facilities, student numbers and other factors. Hence, unregulated competition between institutions within the same family but with differentiated endowments, can lead to unfair competition, and has led to brain gain in one institution in the same country at the expense of another.

On the other extreme has been the case of Rwanda. The Kigali Institute of Science, Technology and Management (KIST) in Rwanda started as a project funded by the UNDP and GTZ and during the period 1995-2002, it recorded a lot of success in terms of attracting a good number of skilled and highly qualified staff both from neighbouring countries and from the Diaspora. In 2002 the government introduced a policy of harmonisation of the public service. When government took over KIST, it continued to pay the same salaries as were paid under the project. This caused feelings of inequity at the National University of Rwanda as its staff felt discriminated. Government reacted by deciding to harmonise service schemes of universities with those of other public services. However, the other agencies such as the Office of the Auditor General, the Pension Fund, the Revenue Authority, the Ministry of Finance, the Tender Board and the state owned enterprises were left with the services and salary structures operating at the time of harmonisation.

When the harmonisation policy was announced, some employees at KIST had loans for vehicles and houses based on the salaries they were earning under the project. All these were affected. It also affected schooling as children had been placed in private schools depending on income. Insurance schemes were also affected. Staff started looking for extra income or alternative jobs. By 2006, about 40 senior staff had left, most of them going to state-owned organisations. The policy change came at a time KIST was gearing up to make bigger contributions to Rwanda's development in the area of IT having started a programme to support IT in schools. It had also begun engaging in community development programmes that were facilitating the acquisition of technology by various communities in the area of energy.[37] Most of the earlier gains seem bound to be lost under the new policy.

These two cases of Rwanda and Zambia raise key issues that need to be addressed in the long run. The first is how regulation can be used to pull up institutions at the bottom without pulling those at the top to the bottom. The second is whether IHEs would be better off if left to design their own ways of coping with market forces without their hands being tied by harmonisation or similar policies. Members of staff interviewed at KIST felt that if they had been given the challenge of looking for ways of topping up government subsidy in order to maintain their salaries and benefits, they would have managed to retain the old system. The case of the University of Zambia shows that using the same regulations or funding policies for institutions with different characteristics is neither scientific nor administratively fair. Perhaps the ultimate solution is more autonomy for universities in mobilising and managing resources. As has been shown by Babalola, Jayeoba and Okideran (2003), more autonomy in resource mobilisation and management, coupled with labour market de-regulation, have helped universities in Brazil, Chile and Jordan to get out of problems that characterize most African universities today.

4.0. Management issues that undermine reform efforts and lead to staff losses

Capacity gaps in the policy frameworks, lack of funding formula, lack of coordination and weak data and statistical systems, are systemic issues at national

---

[37] See Albert Butare, 2004, 'Income Generating Activities in Higher Education: The Case of Kigali Institute of Science and Technology and Management (KIST), *Journal of Higher Education in Africa*, Vol. 2, Number 3, 37-54

and regional levels that deprive higher education institutions of the support they need to be able to deliver on their mandates and have contributed to the aggravation of brain drain. The second set of limitations relates to internal leadership and management processes in the institutions themselves.

4.1.   Infrastructure

Infrastructure in terms of office accommodation and equipment has a big influence on office space, classroom size, research facilities and working conditions generally. Within most HEIs in West, East and Central Africa, infrastructure has deteriorated over a long time and this is one of the causes that job satisfaction is low. Lack of decent, respectable and quality accommodation, has been identified by Sawyerr (2002: 24), and Tettey (2006: 32) as a problem affecting morale and job satisfaction in many tertiary institutions because of over-crowding in offices, classes and laboratories and scarcity of residential accommodation. Added to heavy teaching loads and inadequate teaching materials and equipment, overcrowding is undermining morale and job satisfaction. Some universities have turned to the private sector to look for new avenues of resolving the space and facilities shortage.

The University of Ilorin in Nigeria, for example, has invited private sector organisations to support the construction of new classrooms and a library. Public universities have a tradition of resisting this approach because they feel it may undermine their academic identity and freedom. The Ghana Institute of Management and Public Administration (GIMPA) however, has taken a different route by raising funds through bank loans to construct new classrooms, a library and a conference centre, and it has managed to pay the loan in record time. This has been made possible by the ability of GIMPA to use revenues accruing from its teaching and research contracts to pay the loan on monthly basis. In many HEIs today, the revenues accruing them are enough to enable them not only to raise and repay such loans in time, but also to raise the wages of their staff. The only elements necessary are proper accountability for these revenues and strategic leadership.

Another option is to allow private companies to construct hostels and other facilities on campus and charge user fees at affordable rates. In many public tertiary education institutions, there has been reluctance to allow private or even public enterprises to set up hostels or canteens on campus even where they own large tracts of unutilised land.[38] While reluctance to allow public and private developers continues, the illegal occupation of university land by squatters and unauthorised people is not uncommon.[39] IHEs that are keen on reforms need to develop new policies on private – public and public- public partnerships.

4.2.   Quality of students

Although this issue is affected by systemic factors at national level, it is also affected by management policies at institutional level. In addition, it has impact on the image of HEIs and it affects staff self esteem and job satisfaction. The quality of students has declined (Tettey 2006: 33-34) and this is perpetuating image and credibility problems among academics especially those who do not want to be linked with low standards. Members of the public however, tend to blame the quality of students on the quality of teaching in IHEs, whereas these institutions blame it on poor systems of education delivery and inflation of grades at secondary school level. The University of Namibia, for example, has tried to tackle this problem by launching two-year remedial courses aimed at upgrading possible entrants into its science, medicine and engineering courses. Through this 'access programme' it manages to remedy the problems created in the pre-university training programmes. It has also established a foundation that mobilises resources to support what it terms 'foundation courses' for possible entrants into university programmes in social and natural sciences. It should be noted that some countries in Southern Africa have 12 instead of 14 years of schooling before entry into higher education institutions. Adding one or two years of remedial training may raise the level of students to that in countries with 14 years of pre-higher education training. Institutions where a shorter period of schooling could be affecting the quality of education, such creative programmes, may help in closing the quality gap. However, the longer term solution lies in addressing the factors that affect quality of education at all levels. Some of these are addressed in section 6.5.

---

[38] A few years back the National Social Security Fund in Tanzania wanted to construct a hostel at the University of Dar Es Salaam, which has large tracts of land, but the university refused and the Fund had to construct a hostel four kilometers away from campus, which is not convenient for students.

[39] At the University of Ghana at Legon, squatters have grabbed some of the land allocated to the university.

Box 1: *Academic Staff Views on Why UNZA Loses Staff*

---

a) *Poor working conditions*
   - Remuneration is very low and even when it is increased such measures come too late when rates are already higher in other sectors including some government agencies. o No incentives: the medical scheme is very basic. It does not cover major problems including surgery. o Housing: After 1999 when the houses of university were sold, those who did not benefit from the sale of these houses felt that UNZA would never give them opportunity to become homeowners.
   - Loans: Many institutions in Zambia give their employees loans for cars, houses, furniture etc. UNZA does not have enough funds to give for such loans. If one can get such loans elsewhere, they do not see reason to stay with UNZA.

b) *Instability in the University*
   - Instability in the university has also been a cause for staff turnover. Academics with reputation outside the university don't want to be associated with the instability at the university.

c) *Poor Working Environment*
   - Lack of basic tools and materials to work with also leads to low job satisfaction. Some members of staff feel they subsidise the university by buying their own basic books that should be available in the library or depending on their own computers or accessing internet at their own cost.

d) *Equipment*
   - Not all members of staff have computers. In the Department of Development Studies for example, all got computers in 2007. Projectors, transparencies, flip charts etc., are not easy to access for normal classroom teaching.

e) *Internet Access*
   - While demand for internet services for research and other purposes has increased, the software has not been upgraded for a long time and congestion in the system is chronic.

f) *Delivery in Classrooms*
   - Facilities are still limited. Handouts can no longer be distributed to students. Photocopying is very difficult.

---

g) *Space*
    • UNZA lacks a modern environment in terms of space. Offices are shared and congested. Some offices are leaking and in some, carpets have not been changed for decades.

h) *Upward Mobility*
    • Theoretically promotion is supposed to be automatic upon qualification through publications. But in practice, the university has no money to support the necessary research to encourage publication by its staff. As many cannot publish, they stagnate and after sometime decide to leave.

i) *Staff Development*
    • The staff development programme is not well developed and not well funded and once members of staff remain without further training at Ph.D. level long they cannot advance and tend to look for places where with their qualifications they can get senior positions and better pay.

j) *Contract Research*
    • UNZA does not get big contracts for research. Many institutions lack confidence in the university because of the image of instability. Also issues of accountability for donor funds have impeded efforts to acquire bigger and more contracts.

k) *Treatment for those on staff development*
    • Those on training seem to receive very little help as they prepare to go; while they are on training, as they prepare to come back and after they return. Some are forgotten as soon as they leave and their families abandoned as salary payment is frozen during the period of training.

4.3.   The management of research and staff advancement

The management of research is another issue identified by researchers and staff interviewed as undermining the capacity of higher education institutions to support staff development and career mobility. In all universities visited during this study and contrary to explicit policy guidelines, it seems that implicit policy on promotion puts most of the weight on publications. But without funding of research, career advancement is left to those who can manage to do research on their own or through consultancies. As was shown above, members of staff interviewed during this study were of the opinion that it is dishonest for higher education institutions and accreditation bodies to set high standards of academic advancement when they know that research is the key and it is not adequately funded. Research management, as a factor in capacity retention, goes beyond promotion. In the absence of funding, research in most higher education institutions tends to be individualised. While in certain disciplines, such as history or law, there is no tradition of group research, in science, engineering and medicine, research is best done in groups as it requires shared equipment and materials that cannot be accessed or acquired on individual basis. Besides, group work and exchange of ideas within groups, enriches the quality of research (Becher 1989: 271, Kekäle 2000: 477).Individualisation of research activities creates the problem of winners and losers when criteria for career advancement are uniform for all groups but support is minimal.

Together with research funding and management, is the issue of *promotion and staff advancement*. While all the seven institutions studied have clear promotion procedures and all try as much as possible to abide by them, a few factors cause delays and other problems. First is the centralisation of promotion decisions. In all the seven institutions, promotions are centralised within the institutions in that for all levels, from lectureships to professorships, decisions are taken centrally. While this is necessary for quality assurance, one would expect decisions relating to lower levels to be taken at faculty or college level and submitted for approval to the central administration for quality control. This is not the case and procedures take very long as administrators involved are very busy with other chores. The average decision-making takes from three months to one year and in some cases people leave before decisions are taken or communicated to them. The other dimension of centralised decision-making is where decisions are centralised at national level. In the case of Rwanda, as is the practice in some francophone countries after the centralised procedure at university level is completed, recommendations for promotion are sent to Ministry of Education, which has its own procedures and makes recommendations to the Prime Minister who after consulting Cabinet makes a decision on the recommendations. The procedure could take up to two years.

Box 2: *Reasons for Loss of Staff at the National University of Rwanda According to Interviewed Staff*

System Specific Factors

a) *Excessive government control on travel:* to travel for a conference, the permission of the Prime Minister's Office is required and an application has to be channelled through university administration, MoE to PMO[40]. Decisions take long and sometimes by the time permission is obtained the conference has

---

[40] MoE is Ministry of Education and PMO is Prime Minister's Office

ended. Without that permission no travel authority is possible and no visa can be issued.

b) **Government control of promotions:** under the public service law, the PM is the authority that gives promotion. The recommendation is channelled by the department to the faculty, to the Board of Directors, to the Ministry of Education and from there to the Prime Minister's Office from where the proposal goes to Cabinet. As a result, the procedure takes long and review of academics for promotion is not an annual event like in other universities. It takes place over a period of years.

c) **Comparative Incomes:** In Rwanda, academic staff constitutes the most qualified group in the country, but their salaries are low compared with employees in parastatal organisation and government agencies. In some of these staff with one degree earn twice as much as professors. The Director General of the Rwanda Revenue Authority, for example earns 3 mi RF [41] per month in addition to benefits. Academics have meagre salaries and no benefits.

d) **Working conditions:** some academic staff do not have enough office space to allow them to work comfortably; some have no computers and connectivity is not good. Although NUR has computer laboratories, the number of facilities is not commensurate with that of potential users.

e) **Corporate personality:** although the university is a legal entity, its employees are regarded as government employees and the argument is that no special treatment can be extended to NUR alone.

Management Related Factors

f) **Career development:** facilities for promoting research and support for career development and international recognition are limited.

g) **Staff development:** there is no staff development policy and as a result there are no staff development funds. For administrative staff, there are courses offered by the UNESCO for public administration, but they are occasional and not planned well. The courses offered are too short and what is required is longer training to build capacity for management. There is an assumption that administrators do not need training.

h) Lack of training programmes for administrative staff: it is assumed administrative staff do not require serious training. The short courses they are given do not impart critical skills.

---

[41] RF is Rwandese francs

4.4.   Job satisfaction and the management of perceptions

Job satisfaction is now becoming very crucial in human resources management in public and private institutions as the competition for talents intensifies. In knowledge intensive institutions such as those of higher education, to maintain appropriate levels of employee job satisfaction requires actual and constant awareness of the labour force characteristics, the changing value systems in these institutions and how to measure and improve job satisfaction. The study sought to find out, in the first place, if the management in the institutions visited had any personnel policies. What were available in all of them were personnel management manuals spelling out procedures for recruitment, advancement and allocating benefits and loans. Much as these are positive instruments that standardise personnel management, there is still need for personnel policies covering issues that go beyond procedures, spelling out policies and strategies for identifying the right personnel, policies on how to improve job satisfaction and modify the behaviour of staff in order to get the best out them.

In the study, some questions were raised on core values and how they are integrated in human resources management in the six institutions. As they shape perceptions of work and organisational commitment, management officials were asked about these values and if they feature in their human resources management strategies. Questions were raised around the major principles through which these values are normally expressed. The first principle focused upon was utilitarianism and egalitarianism. This value is upheld by most organisations and it is expressed by the constant wish and effort of academic institutions to secure the best results for the majority of staff.

This principle when applied in big organisations such as those of higher education, it takes a group approach to issues and motivation structures. Hence, systems apply to all without differentiation, sometimes to avoid what may be regarded as negative discrimination. Applying the principles of utilitarianism and egalitarianism and deliberately avoiding differentiation, all members of academic staff are treated from the same perspective. For example:
-    All are assumed and expected to be good researchers and good teachers. This ignores the fact that not all good teachers are good researchers and that while it is most appropriate for good teachers to be good researchers, some are good teachers and have little inclination for research or writing, while some have good research and writing skills, but are weak on teaching or oral communication of ideas.
-    The needs of all academics are assumed to be the same or similar and they are all assumed to be capable of competing at the same level. But single parents, elderly members who may have been surpassed by the IT revolution, young

academics with limited networking experience or physically challenged staff who are differently able (d)[42], cannot compete with those with less extra curricula chores, or more socially or technologically connected or those with more networking experience.

-    Motivation strategies such as increments and other fringe benefits are assumed to be capable of working in the same way for all employees. This may ignore the cross-cultural variables that shape perceptions of motivational factors such as individualism versus collectivism (Niles 1998), utilitarianism versus normativism[43] and achieved as opposed to ascribed status.[44]

-    Salaries are assumed compensate all at the same level. This ignores that fact that monetary compensation does not cover the differentiated contributions of individual members of staff in critical areas of the institution's mandate. It also ignores the fact that academic institutions compete for the energy and commitment of their staff with external agencies such as the private sector, private practice, and political, civil society and spiritual organisations etc.

Such assumptions that underlie the principles of utilitarianism and egalitarianism as value systems are no longer handy for knowledge organisations that are competing on capabilities with bigger and better resourced institutions within and outside the continent. Differentiated treatment and in some cases, special group treatment and individualised packages, are more practical than bandwagon incentive schemes and income policies. Although a good number of HEIs are moving towards differential treatment of individual contributions and capabilities and where necessary, developing group or individual packages to allow themselves to compete with outside agencies for special skills and competencies, egalitarianism still constrains reforms in reward systems.

---

[42] The term 'differently abled' is used instead of the conventional term 'disabled', which fails to recognize the different endowments of the challenged people.

[43] People with utilitarian values tend to focus on short terms and immediate gains while people with normative orientation study the norms in organizations and strive to follow them and succeed within them in the long term. The two groups perceive motivational strategies differently.

[44] Some people derive satisfaction from titles and symbols of power especially if they give them influence and recognition. Others are motivated by achieved status, which they earn through hard work and competitive advantage over others.

[45] Prof. Agyeman Badu is the Deputy Rector of the Ghana Institute of Management and Public Administration. He expressed these views in an interview with the author on the 1st August 2007.

Box 3: Why higher education institutions still lose staff:
A view from Prof. Agyeman Badu[45]

a) **Conditions of Service:** have remained almost the same for decades and universities have got used to them so much that they see them as normal.

b) **Infrastructure:** has deteriorated so much and no efforts have been made to rehabilitate it.

c) **Pay systems:** are lagging behind industry and in some cases other government agencies.

d) **Aging faculty:** still in control, conservative and too used to the situation to see anything wrong with it.

e) Poor management: universities have not been good at practicing what they preach, good management and good governance.

f) Quality of education: when academics are associated with poor quality of education which they have no influence or power to change, they become disillusioned and go.

g) Government policies: many governments still look at universities as other public institutions of service. They do not see them as key producers of knowledge that is essential for economic and social transformation.

h) **Change management:** universities teach and preach change management to others but rarely try to put it into practice.

i) **Poor lobbying skills:** in many countries all leaders have passed through the few existing universities. In theory universities should be on top of every organisation because they have alumni in all public institutions. But they take this social capital for granted.

j) **Refusing to bring in private developers:** most public universities have large tracts of land that was allocated to them while the governments were still very generous. Most of this land is un-utilised.

Individual and group rights constitute another set of ethical values that shape perceptions of institutions about services and entitlements. An institution's sense of justice is determined by its codification and application of ethical practices that ensure that rights of individuals are respected. Most HEIs have spelt these out clearly in their strategic plans as core values. Some members of staff interviewed in the seven institutions thought that the values about rights were weak in their institutions and that the low perceptions of staff about rights and entitlements were causing decline in morale and job satisfaction. The problem is more manifest in the divide between local and expatriate staff. In Rwanda for example, the differences in income for the two groups are so big that they make very little sense when one looks at the chores and contributions made by people with similar contributions from different groups. In the case of the University of Botswana from another extreme example, preferential treatment of local staff over expatriate staff in terms of benefits, has caused dissatisfaction among foreign staff (Tettey 2006). In both extremes, the way individual and group rights are managed can easily cause job dissatisfaction and lead to search for alternative employment.

Finally, to strengthen these core values, higher education institutions need to develop strategies for increasing fairness as a critical factor in job satisfaction. To have committed employees, there is a need to increase fairness in resource distribution. Academics will not remain loyal when they see for example, administrative staff enjoying common facilities such as transport, even after working hours, when it is difficult for them to get such facilities in the performance of their official duties. Similarly, administrative personnel find it difficult to understand why training and staff development are seen as exclusively for academic staff in some universities or why they are rarely supported to attend workshops and seminars. In some institutions relations between academic and administrative staff tend to be frictional because of feelings of inequality and unfairness in the distribution of resources. Distributive justice should be seen as a mechanism for staff motivation and retention.

5.0. The Motivation Revolution in African Institutions of Higher Education

In the last three to five years, after difficult negotiations with governments, some public institutions of higher education have been given leeway to review their salary schemes and introduce new and better incentives for staff. Although in some countries, the new salary scales are still lagging behind the going rates on the market, the mere fact that there has been a review and commitment by the institutions and their governments to raise living standards and make provision for better working conditions, is a big step forward. Below, we examine some of the innovative incentives and salary schemes that have been put in place.

5.1. Innovative Ways of Retaining Staff at the Kwame Nkrumah University of Science and Technology in Ghana

After experiencing considerable depletion of its staff capacity and taking advantage of policy reforms and the willingness of the Ghana government to support innovative salary and incentive schemes in its public universities, the Kwame Nkrumah University of Science and Technology (KNUST) has devised some of the best strategies to attract and retain staff. It tries to tackle multiple issues such as working condition, security of tenure, health and social security and incomes. Some of the strategies are as follows:

Land Distribution
The University has acquired land and is selling pieces of it to members of staff to enable them to build houses. The conditions for allocation are that a member should

have a tenured position. The land cannot be transferred except with the permission of the University and only to fellow staff members.

Training young members of staff
The KNUST has established a staff development programme under which young members of staff in need of further training are given scholarships locally for training to Ph.D. level. They are paid a stipend and supervision fees are paid to senior staff supervising them. They are exempted from teaching. Leave of absence for staff is allowed and where they cannot get scholarships.

Creativity and talent management
Achievement is recognized and where possible rewarded. The VC recognizes and announces achievers of the year annually. Besides, the University has a mechanical engineering project, which it runs in collaboration with the University of North Carolina. Students assemble cars and test them. Several cars have been assembled. Commercialisation of these cars is underway in partnership with the private sector.

Investing in infrastructure
The University has invested over US$ 35 million in the refurbishment of laboratories. This has covered 27 labs in the colleges of science. Also library facilities have been introduced and inter-library loan systems used to cover the shortfall in books.

Coordinating research
Research is inter-departmental. The Technology Consultancy Centre (TCC) coordinates inter-departmental research. All departments working on similar projects such as energy, link up under the Centre.

Continuous medical check ups
The university runs a medical centre with eight doctors, a fully equipped laboratory and has a health insurance scheme, and since 2006 it has introduced a voluntary testing scheme for hypertension, diabetes and colonoscopy. It has also introduced counselling facilities aimed at stress management.

Balancing teaching and research
Teaching and research are weighted equally in management and performance evaluation. To support teaching a quality assurance planning unit was set up to assess teaching and design teaching and learning improvement programmes. Young faculty are encouraged to undergo training in teaching methods and are given administrative responsibilities such as management of halls of residence as Hall Tutors. Students evaluate teaching and submit reports. All these help staff to improve teaching, gain confidence and increase their job satisfaction.

Shortening recruitment procedures

The KNUST has developed a procedure of head hunting staff for senior positions. While the average period of recruitment is about 8 months in Ghana, KNUST has shortened procedures and the whole procedure takes approximately a month.

5.2. The New Salary and Incentive Schemes at the University of Zambia (UNZA)[46]

Table 1: **UNZA New Salary and Benefit Scheme of (2007)**

a) New Salary Scheme	
Lecturer 3	6,740,000 per month -30-35% tax
Lecturer 2	7,533,000 –do
Lecturer 1	8,587,000 –do-
Senior Lecturer	9,751,000 –do-
Associate Professor	11,182,000 –do-
Profe ssor	12,970,000 –do-
b) Housing Allowance	
Based on seniority	1.6 mi kwacha per month
Professional Staff	1.3 mi kwacha per month
Technical Staff	Paid directly to landowner
Owner Occupier Allowance	800,000 kwacha per month for academic staff 650,000 kw acha for technical staff
c) Other Allowance	
Excess teaching load	Teaching in excess of 2 courses or 75 or more students
Settling Allowance	2mi kwacha on recruitment
Non -Private Practice Allowance	1.2 mi p.a. (Law, Engineering and Medicine)
Clinical Al lowance	1mi. p.a. (Medicine and Vet)
Course Coordination	1 mi per semester
Field Allowance	65,000 kwacha per day
Retention Allowance	130,000 kwacha per month
Terminal Packages	Death, Gratuity and Retirement-service tied

Exchange rate: 1 US$ = 3,860 Kwacha as of August 5th 2007

Retirement/ Terminal Benefits

1-3 Years of Service	4 months salary x number of years worked
4-7 Years of Service	19 months salary
8-10 Years of Service	24 months salary
11-20 Years of Service	4 months salary x number of years served
Over 20 Years of Service	5 months salary x number of years served

---

[46] It would have been better to get the previous salary scheme for UNZA but due to communication bottlenecks this was no possible.

38

Retirees: Retain house until benefits are paid in full

Group Life Insurance Scheme
24 Hours Cover
Group Personal Accident 3 x One's Annual salary for each
Injury As determined by doctors- all accidents

Superannuation Scheme
Contribution by Staff 6%
Contribution by the University 17%
Full benefits on retirement at 55 or death

Sabbatical Leave
One year of Sabbatical leave on full pay

Incentive Scheme for Technical and Senior Administrative Staff
Superannuation
Housing payable to landowners
Special Leave without pay to work elsewhere
Subscription to professional organizations

5.3. Measures Aimed at Retaining Staff at the University of Cape Coast, Ghana

Accommodation:	Provided for all staff
Loan Scheme:	Owner occupier allowance for home owners
	Out of campus allowance
	Car maintenance loans for car owners
	Salary advance
	Car purchase loans
	Refridgerator loans
	Furniture loans
	Loan guarantee schemes
Allowances:	Responsibility allowance for leadership and management positions
Welfare Benefits:	Staff pension scheme
	Medical services for all staff, their spouses and up to six children.
Awards:	Best worker awards each year
	Long service awards
	Thirteenth month cheque for all at the end of the year

Staff Advancement: Effective staff appraisal system, mentorship and leadership succession plans.

5.4. An Integrated Approach to Motivation at the Ghana Institute of Management and Public Administration

The Ghana Institute of Management and Public Administration (GIMPA) in Ghana is an old IHE that has undergone renewal, and exhibits the new spirit of African IHEs. The leadership and management team have adopted academic entrepreneurship and certain aspects of new public management. The assessment below indicates what has combined in their various approaches to attract staff from other institutions, head hunt and recruit highly qualified Ghanaians from the Diaspora and raise enough resources to reduce their dependency on government subsidies.

a)   Commitment to action
The new management team were recruited with the purpose of changing the situation at GIMPA and responding to a need for capacity building in the area of management. They exhibit a commitment to action and this helps the Institute to obtain results.

b)   Flexible procedures
Quick decisions on recruitment hold the key to adequate responses to labour market competition and meeting the needs of the clients. At GIMPA, the Deans and senior management officials have been given the mandate to locate and enter preliminary negotiations with potential recruits. A senior official on mission or attending a workshop can make a commitment on behalf of the Institute regarding possibilities of employment if such an official comes across a potential or suitable candidate.

c)   Individualised contracts
In case a suitable candidate is identified who cannot be adequately remunerated under the standard salary scales of GIMPA, the Institute has a policy giving such a person personal contract. Such differentiated contracts are also supported by commitments on the part of the recruits to use their experience and networks to acquire strategic resources for the institute.[47]

Differentiated payment systems are possible in many universities. The only problem is that in some they can be easily abused and foster ethnicity and social stratification instead of being used strategically to reward output or as investments for more resources accruing or likely to accrue to the universities.

d)   Commitment to retention of staff

Awareness that tertiary institutions on the continent are engaged in an unfair war for talents with bigger economies has forced GIMPA to look for the best ways to attract and retain staff. In the case of Ghana for example, the whole country has one Ph.D. holder in Computer Science. He was offered a job within one week. He has now been allowed by GIMPA to establish his own private practice on campus while teaching for them. GIMPA has managed through contacts with Ghanaians abroad, alumni networks and advertisements, to head - hunt for senior professionals in the Diaspora, who are ready to come back or work closely with African universities.

e)   Workload management

GIMPA organises its courses in such a way that the workload is intensive during the time programmes are in session, but it allows short breaks in between to allow research and community service.

f)   Retirement age

The age has been extended to 65 and retirees can still work on part-time basis.

g)   New methods of delivery

GIMPA relies very much on ICTs to reduce the problems of class size and workload management. Training staff to use computer-based teaching and research techniques seems to have increased job satisfaction among some staff at GIMPA.

5.5.   Staff Views on Strategies for Enhancing Staff Retention

During the study, it was difficult to organise meetings with academic staff at the Ghana Institute of Management and Public Administration, the University of Ghana, the University of Cape Coast and the Kwame Nkrumah University for Science and Technology because the interviews were exclusively with leaders and managers. At the National University of Rwanda, the Kigali Institute of Science, Technology and Management and the University of Zambia, it was possible to get audience with academic staff and get their views on the problems and the solutions. Below is a summary of their views on what would strengthen the capacity of tertiary institutions across the continent to retain staff.

a)   Enabling incomes

The levels of income should enable staff to access loans from commercial institutions, enrol in secure medical insurance schemes and pay school fees for their children.

b)   Loan guarantee schemes

Loan guarantee schemes can help resolve housing problems and anxiety about life after employment without a retirement home. They can also help staff to buy cars and increase their mobility.

c)   Pension schemes

Insurance schemes are limited and the availability of basic care though appreciated does not suffice when staff require surgery or other expensive health services. Such services require comprehensive medical care insurance opportunities that can become accessible with incomes that are sufficient. HEIs together can approach insurance companies for such schemes and given the numbers of staff in these universities, many private insurers would be attracted to the idea.

d)   Recognition and rewards systems

To avoid recognition systems becoming rituals, they need to be decentralised and organised at faculty level. Otherwise, they will become meaningless tokens serving public relations objectives rather motivation of staff.[48]

e)   Staff development

In spite of resource constraints, there is no short cut to secure staffing levels if training is not given a priority. Staff development is the key to retention of staff, and HEIs that have intensified training do not suffer as much as those that have invested little in it when it comes to staff losses.

f)   Decentralisation and devolution of powers

To facilitate quick and responsive action in recruitment, training and promotion, most powers and decisions need to be delegated to faculties and colleges. Centralisation of power in a competitive globalised economy is a fetter to efficiency and undermines the reforms that universities have undertaken.

g)   Research support

To make staff accountable in teaching and research, it is necessary to provide all with the necessary funds, equipment, materials and time. Otherwise, teaching evaluation, staff assessment and promotion procedures may become arbitrary.

GIMPA has managed to recruit at least five top class Ph.D holders from Germany, the US and the UK. All are Ghanaians. In addition it has recruited senior staff from the Diaspora. They include Prof. Stephen Adei, Rector; Prof Agyeman Badu, Deputy Rector; Prof. Clement Somuah, Dean of the School of Technology; Dr. Josiah Cobbah, Acting Dean , School of Governance and Leadership and Dr. George Appenteng.

h) Support for teaching

While a living wage increases motivation and commitment, job satisfaction is enhanced by conditions that make academic work enjoyable and challenging. Without books, journals, functioning Internet systems and other necessities, work may become a constraint rather than a challenge.

i) Government priorities

Governments need to re-examine the importance of higher education in critical policy initiatives including their development visions and poverty eradication. If they continue to treat tertiary education as secondary matter, those policy initiatives may never take off even with the best of goodwill and support from donors.

j) Donor support

More donor support is required to restore the respect and utility of African institutions of tertiary education. Without strengthening them, problems of the continent will continue to overflow into the economies of developed countries.

k) Inter-University collaboration

Regional and sub-regional bodies have to increase cooperation in resource sharing through staff exchange, joint teaching programmes and collective research and consultancy.

6.0. Redressing the Brain Drain

In the previous section, we have seen what staff at various institutions think should be done to attract and retain human resources in HEIs. The best solution is to increase the pace of economic growth, strengthen democracy and remove systems that encourage social exclusion and ethnic, racial, gender and other types of discrimination. Improved governance could create space for participation of the majority in economic activities and promote wealth creation, which could in turn increase a sense of national and community belonging for many and help generate adequate resources at national level to support investment in education. The duty to improve the economic situation in Africa does not lie on the state alone. Education institutions, government agencies and various sectors and development partners have all a contribution to make.

6.1. State Support for Economic Growth

The wage gap between developed economies and less developed ones has its roots in lack of dynamic growth. At the moment however, economic growth on the continent seems to be steady. According to the OECD African Economic Outlook for 2006

(Kauffmann and Wegner, 2006), the overall growth rate was at an average of 5%, average per capita income was up 3% and inflation was steady at 10%. In the 30 countries surveyed, there was net growth in investments. But in spite of the average figures, there were some worrying trends. The biggest growth was in the mineral sector supported by rise in the prices of oil and oil products. The financial sector was also growing rapidly with all the potential volatility characteristic of financial markets. Agricultural production went down, although it still supports averagely 70% of the continent's population. Some countries most hard hit by brain drain such as Zimbabwe, Cote d'Ivore, Central African Republic and Seychelles had negative growth. In addition, 27 countries including Africa's most promising economies such as Mauritius, Namibia and South Africa had less than average growth.

Seventeen countries, some of which have experienced serious brain drain including DRC, Ethiopia, Sudan and Zambia, recorded high growth rates, but they were not enough to help them come closer to achieving the Millennium Development Goals. Only seven countries (Tanzania, Nigeria, Mozambique, Sierra Leone, Angola, Chad and Equatorial Guinea) had very high growth rates but significantly, these are countries with a very narrow manufacturing base, the majority are mineral or single commodity dependent economies and over half of them are either emerging from conflict or still threatened by internal strife. These trends do not give basis for an optimistic picture of the development trends. Fluctuations have in the past been a norm with the best performers in one year retreating in performance the following years. While the achievements made in the last decade should not be dismissed, there is a need to continue efforts to increase growth.

One major problem that receives limited attention is the transport system. Sub-Saharan Africa significantly remains a donkey, canoe and footpath based economy apart from a few roads leading to places where the elite hail from or mining and other strategic centres. Goldestein and Kauffmann (2005-6) have indicated that Sub-Saharan Africa accounts for only 3% of the world rail transport; in 1999 about 10% of the global road accidents took place in Sub-Saharan Africa, although the total share of Sub-Sahara Africa in the global road network is very small. They estimated that only 4.5% of air traffic is in Africa, but its share of air traffic accidents was 25% in 2004. To be able to facilitate the exploitation of the immense natural resources the continent is endowed with, there is a need to invest in the transport infrastructure, conduct research on alternative transport systems, look for ways of reducing dependency on roads and adequately using rivers and other water resources for transport, investing in ports, dredging them and making full use of them and generally allowing easy movement of people and goods in order to increase trade and services.

6.2. Promoting Peace, Security and Stability

The recent experience in Zimbabwe is a clear example of the significance of peace in economic and social development. The impact of open or latent conflict on migration and brain drain can be seen not only from the actual losses suffered by countries such as Zimbabwe (Chikanda, 2005) or Sierra Leone, Liberia, DRC or Cape Verde as shown earlier, but also from the expressed intentions of students in colleges to leave their countries and if possible for good, immediately after graduation! Distress levels and anxiety to leave after graduation in Southern African countries including those not yet experiencing disruption or open conflicts is very alarming. A study by Crush, Pendelton and Tevera (2005) in six Southern African countries indicated that 50% of university students were thinking of leaving their countries after graduation, and 25% of them were thinking of staying away for longer than two years.

In a separate study by Tevera (2005) on Zimbabwean students, 71.2% said they were contemplating moving abroad immediately after graduation, 32% had already applied for residence rights abroad, 62.3% were thinking of migrating to Europe, North America, Australia and New Zealand and 36.1% to other countries in Southern Africa. In all cases, restlessness, anxiety about economic and social stability, land, job and livelihoods security, availability and affordability of health and education services for their children and political stability, were outlined as the main causes for their intentions to migrate. If therefore these young people have to be won over or if those who migrated have to be encouraged to return, peace, security and stability have to be transformed into an every day reality.

6.3. Investing More in Education

It is no longer debatable that investments in higher education carry high rates of returns, raise levels of educational attainment, prepare citizens for lifelong learning, promote creativity, technology acquisition and diffusion and improve governance. A joint ENESCO-OECD survey of 19 middle-income countries has revealed that from 1980 to 2000, increases in investments in human capital development accounted for over 0.5% in annual growth rates in these countries; private returns on further education were considerable as people with tertiary education in Indonesia, for example, were earning 82% more than those with secondary education; as years of schooling in Chile doubled between 1960 and 2000, the GDP also doubled, while in Malaysia during the same period, years of schooling trebled and the GDP trebled too. (UNESCO/OECD: 2003).

Recent studies on less developed countries in Africa have also shown that the level of education affects household per capita consumption, family size, access to education and other social services and capability to earn a decent income (Burkina Faso PRSP

2004: 28). A combination of advanced human capital development and proper governance has been proved to impact on trade, investment, productivity and technological development (Teal 2001, 2003) and it has been shown that growth in living standards and poverty eradication were fastest for more educated households and increased chances for household members to earn more in employment, non-agricultural activities and in self employment (Appeleton 2001). Less investment in education even in the rural or marginalised sectors in middle-income countries tends to lead to reduction in growth and sustains structures of poverty and vulnerability (Francis, 2006). Therefore, using personal returns indicators such as entry into labour markets, learning capability, diffusion of knowledge and technology, entry into and survival in income-generating activities, it is not a moot issue that investing in higher education yields high dividends. Countries that have managed to reverse the brain drain and enter the category of those who are experiencing brain exchange such as Malaysia, Singapore, Chile and Israel have managed to reach that status because of heavy investments in education.

6.4. Creating capacity to Learn within Higher Education Institutions

While almost everyone is talking about Africa joining the knowledge society, very little debate or thinking has gone into how this can be attained. Africa was bypassed by the first green revolution, it is likely to be bypassed by the second green or the so-called 'evergreen'[49] revolution and it is lagging behind in the information revolution. Higher education institutions in partnership with government agencies and international development partners can combine efforts to bridge the glaring gap between hope, hype and reality. The reality is that the pace for building capacity for African countries to join the information and knowledge society is very slow. As Hargrieves and Shaw (2005), have argued, bridging the gap between what they call current realties and the desired future, requires capabilities to create, use, circulate and adopt knowledge. To do that, they insist, requires the creation of a knowledge economy based on technology learning. To create conditions for becoming part of the knowledge economy, a culture of lifelong learning needs to be adopted by HEIs through which staff will be equipped with state-of –the-art skills to acquire and share knowledge. Provision of up-to-date, affordable, accessible and functioning IT systems and packages is crucial. There are numerous databases in natural sciences, medicine, engineering, economics and law that most staff are not exposed to or unable to access. Capability to access them can improve knowledge and innovation and support dissemination of such knowledge.

---

[49] The evergreen revolution is emphasizing using biotechnology in an environmentally conscious way, using clean technologies, observing bio-safety and bio-ethics standards and using materials that have a potential for solving multiple problems for example food, feed and fuel .

Currently, HEIs are doing a lot to get themselves connected, overcome bandwidth problems and reduce the cost of Internet. But they need to go further. To join the global knowledge communities, skills upgrading is essential, training and lifelong learning crucial and application of knowledge critical. Currently, some innovation centres in Ghana, Kenya , Tanzania and Uganda for example, within HEIs have confined their R&D activities to the provision of technical and brokerage services to SMEs and have remained somehow dominated by the appropriate technology approaches that keep them engaged in simple technologies that now even small-scale enterprises are capable of manufacturing (Enos 1995). To move out of these traditional confines, innovation centres in HEIs need to develop capacity to acquire, generate, apply and disseminate advanced knowledge. They have to take lead in developing new science and technology policies for their countries as the first generation of these policies developed in the 1980s has become obsolete and irrelevant. To enable themselves to take lead in research and development, they have to design long-term multi-disciplinary research programmes that will enable them to team up with state-based research organisations and the private sector. This will enable them to shift from individualised to collective research, increase knowledge sharing, resources pooling, equipment sharing and formation of consortia for contact research. If well organised and if they abandon individualised and personalised research approaches, research can become an engine for growth within these institutions and promote the quality of outcomes and impact on economic development.

6.5.   Improving the Quality of Education and Creating an Educated Workforce

The impact of the low quality of education on the standing of African HEIs and the image problems associated with it cannot be left to HEIs alone. State institutions and HEIs have a joint responsibility to redress the problems. The quality problem stems from poorly resourced, badly managed, over-crowded school systems at primary and secondary level. In some countries, the education budget is sizeable, but the quality of education is not improving. Studies carried out about a decade ago indicated that reading culture was very low among primary school pupils in Ghana and Benin, writing skills were below average in Mali and Togo and oral communication was not well advanced in Benin and Cameroon (Maclure 1997: 32-33). Insufficient reading and writing practice, disorganised systems of teaching, staff turnover and mobility, absence of a reading culture at home, overcrowded classrooms, lack of lifelong education programmes for teachers, dependence on rote teaching methods, lack of feedback from teachers to pupils and parents, were some of the systemic factors that impeded and still impede learning in many schools on the continent.

Recent poverty reduction strategy papers of several countries such as Burkina Faso, Burundi, Cameroon, and Malawi indicate that there are high repetition rates, classroom sizes are still very big, achievement rates are rising for pupils in urban areas and declining for those in rural areas, girls in rural areas are still behind in terms of access, completion rates and achievement rates. Special problems affecting girls in schools such as housework versus homework; adolescent bonding, girl child kidnapping, elopement and early entry into marriage; puberty myths, sexual rituals and cultural indoctrination through taboos, rites of passage and other cultural practices etc., are undermining the capacity of girls to achieve and develop at the same level as boys in certain communities. (UNESCO 2003/4: 115-135) These problems are being carried into secondary schools, vocational education systems and ultimately higher education institutions.

For governments and their development partners that have argued for over three decades that the best sector to invest in is the basic education sub-sector and indeed having poured resources into this sub-sector, the persistence of learning problems at this level and their spill over into higher levels, calls for a holistic approach. An approach that strengthens all the sub-sectors from early childhood education to primary, secondary, vocational and technical to higher education, because each of these sub-sectors affects the others vertically and horizontally. The 2002 *Global EFA Monitoring Report* has provided a comprehensive framework for assessing education quality, focusing on inputs covering school, student characteristics, households and community factors; process factors such as school climate, teaching and learning and contextual factors and outcomes such as cognitive development, attainment and standards.(UNESCO 2002: 81). On the other hand, HEIs owe it to themselves to strive to create an educated, responsive, knowledgeable, innovative, agile, flexible, transparent and ethical labour force that can help African economies to move, give HEIs and Africa a good name and help African public and private institutions to become more efficient and competitive. Without making an effort to create such a labour force, the economies will not grow fast enough to finance the education systems adequately or help HEIs to retain the necessary human resources.

6.6.   Supporting Returnee Programmes

6.6.1.   The Experience of TOKTEN and RQAN

Over the last 15 years, the UNDP, IOM and bilateral development partners have invested substantially in efforts to assist willing migrants abroad to come back to Africa and strengthen the capacity of mainly public institutions. The UNDP established the Transfer of Knowledge Through Expatriate Nationals (TOKTEN) in 1983 aimed at replacing expatriate workers in African countries by national with similar or better qualifications. In addition, the IOM launched the Return of Qualified African Nationals (RQAN) also in 1983 to help highly qualified African experts to return to African countries on voluntary basis. In addition to being very costly and therefore inherently unsustainable, the two programmes did not get enough local support Although close to 2000 such nationals were helped to return to the continent, these initiatives were not as successful as had been anticipated. A number of problems were behind this limited success.

First, they were viewed in many African countries as donor driven and mainly aimed at repatriating African experts to satisfy the anti-migration constituencies in the North. Second, the underlying motives and thinking ignored the globalisation trends in scientific mobility supported by the presence of multinational corporations, value chains in production and services and higher education links and networks. Third, there was an unfounded assumption that experts on the ground would happily receive the returnees and integrate them easily. Fourth, the initiatives ignored the push factors that had made the experts leave in the first place and were pushing others out of the continent. For example, due to ethnic and racial tensions in some countries, expatriates are seen by the local elite as a solution, because they tend to have no political or social affiliations. Finally, local leaders have learnt from history that returnees or émigrés tend to bring with them radical ideas that in some cases have helped to bring revolution. Such leaders have the potential for being cautious at best and hostile at the worst to returnees. As a result of these and other factors, RQAN has been replaced by a less ambitious programme, the Migration for Development in Africa (MIDA) aimed at linking up African institutions with professionals in the Diaspora without relocating them to the continent.

6.6.2. MIDA in Ghana

MIDA in Ghana seeks to mobilise knowledge, skills, networks and experiences of Ghanaian Migrant Professors (GMPs) and tailor them to the needs and priorities of tertiary education institutions in Ghana, to utilise e-learning centres for the facilitation of transfer of knowledge by skilled GMPs in the US, Canada and the UK to students in tertiary institutions in Ghana and generally to promote cooperation between tertiary institutions in Ghana and the Ghanaian Diaspora (MIDA Project Document). The project has four components. The first one covers the creation of awareness and establishment of a database on GMPs. The second one is needs assessment at selected Ghanaian HEIs. The third is facilitation of transfer of knowledge through support of migrants to return temporarily to Ghana and take part in the activities of Ghanaian HEIs. The fourth is initiation of virtual learning programmes between GMPs and Ghanaian HEIs. In this component is the specific use of GIMPA's e-learning centre for virtual learning programmes. MIDA has programmes in other African countries, but not all specialise on academic migrants and for the purposes of this report, the discussion is confined to Ghana.

To avoid problems of local ownership, the project has local partners that have been involved in all stages of its formation and have an equal say with IOM in decision making. They are IOM Ghana, Ministry of foreign Affairs in Ghana, Ministry of Education in Ghana, Ghana Diaspora organisations in targeted countries, i.e. Canada, the UK and the US and the US, UK, Canadian and Japanese governments. Conspicuously missing from the list of partners is the Association of Ghana Vice Chancellors. Although MIDA Ghana has just started its activities, it has already attracted GMPs to work in Ghana's teaching hospitals and some have been working with local authorities on health issues. As mentioned above, HEIs are not involved in the decision making mechanism. A selected number of them will be invited to take part in the programme by making teaching positions available for GMPs and provide them with accommodation and logistical support. In the long term however, this is likely to weaken the local ownership of the programme, because the main actors and beneficiaries are given a recipient role. Some of the leaders interviewed at the University of Ghana did not seem to have confidence that GMPs were genuine about coming back to give support to HEIs. They thought that more often than not, they were motivated by personal interest such as coming back temporarily, while waiting for renewal of their visas. In the view of the author, this should not be a consideration in the utilisation of the GMPs, because what matters is their contribution no matter why they come back to the country. But lack of full involvement on the part of the HEIs leaders will continue to alienate them from the purpose and effect of the programme. Further initiatives for linking with the Diaspora are discussed in the next section.

7.0.   Linking up with the Diaspora

At the Africa Development Forum meeting on 'The Role of the African Digital Diaspora in Enhancing ICT Development in Africa' in September (13-19) 1999, a presentation was made on the potential of the Diaspora to contribute to Africa's development. While willingness on the part of the Diaspora to do that was unmistakable, there were some feelings on the part of some policy makers and a number of local experts that most of the experts in the Diaspora were only interested in working in their own countries and not simply any country in Africa (ECA 1999). Some even thought that the Diaspora experts were opportunists who left when the conditions were unbearable on the continent and wanted to return when those who remained had managed to reduce these problems.[50]

---

[50] Some universities in Ghana have had some cases where members of the Diaspora expressed interest in coming back, were accepted back only to leave after a short time going back to their host countries. In most of these cases the Diaspora wanted to use the interval to get their residence permits renewed. Some of these experiences also increased the suspicions of local institutions.

At the First Conference of Intellectuals of Africa and the Diaspora held in Dakar 6-9 October 2004, it was crystal clear that the reservations expressed at the 1999 conference had been replaced by enthusiasm and zeal about the role of the Diaspora in Africa's development. It was recommended among other things that 20 Diaspora organisations existing then would be part of the ECOSOCC of the AU; that a representative body of these organisations should be established and that the Diaspora should be constituted into the sixth region of the AU (AU, 2004:14). More far reaching recommendations at the conference called for the creation by the AU of a secretariat to engage in a dialogue between African intellectuals, policy makers and the Diaspora; establishment by the AU of an agency to promote Africa's interests abroad and promote commercial and other links between the Diaspora and Africa and development of a new curriculum council to facilitate the development and dissemination of literature for Africa and the Diaspora. Also prominent was the recommendation to establish a framework for African citizenship and an African passport. (AU, 2004: 21-22)

There is increasing realisation that there is a global process of decentralisation of services and production and relocation of these to economies where costs are lower. As multinational operations seek to decentralise, they are looking for knowledge workers who have technical skills and added advantages of knowledge of the languages and cultures of their intended markets and the Diaspora are gaining competitive advantage on these added factors. Hence, experts in the Diaspora are being targeted by such organisations for deployment in new markets where they can help them to function better in new environments. In this context it is necessary for African countries to see the Diaspora as knowledge workers who can help them in their difficult struggle to attract investments and enter the knowledge society.

In the area of higher education, changes that have made the Diaspora very crucial in Africa's development are taking place. In the first place, higher education institutions and policies in Europe and North America have undergone fundamental reforms in the last 20 years, processes, which have enriched the technical skills of the Diaspora on higher education policy, management and delivery. The processes of education reform that have started on the continent can be greatly enriched by this experience. In addition the liberalisation of trade in services including those in higher education, is leading to a push by developed country's higher education institutions to establish campuses in Africa and compete directly with African universities. In the ensuing competition, it is becoming clear that developed country's institutions are using the African Diaspora to develop courses and even run them on the continent, given the competitive advantages they have as discussed above.

In the process, African governments and universities are being left with two choices: either to forge alliances with the Diaspora and utilise their skills or to leave those skills to be further used by developed country's higher education institutions in the ensuing competition against them. As the process of cross-border delivery intensifies, it will be a matter of who mobilises the Diaspora first and best. In addition, some universities that are thinking of North-South partnerships in the delivery of higher education services are finding the Diaspora very resourceful as they help to connect them with the right institutions, develop courses for these joint programmes and even manage them and become link persons between the partner institutions.[51] The choice for African countries has increasingly become whether they should allow the Diaspora to work with them as allies or against them as allies of their rivals on the education market.[52]

Kuznetsov (2006) has identified six methods in which Diaspora resources have been integrated or utilised in their countries of origin worldwide. The first method is the one that was used by India, which managed to get top executives of Indian origin in multinational corporations abroad to lobby for relocation of high tech industries to India or secure outsourcing contracts to Indian's high tech firms. This was behind the 'Indian miracle' that has seen India becoming a player in the ICT revolution. Kutznetsov and Sabel (2006:15) have cautioned however, that, 'The emergence of the Indian software industry was in some ways a fortunate accident that almost surely cannot be reproduced by other countries. But it was an accident waiting to happen depending on the structural condition that can indeed be influenced by policy. The Indian government's emphasis on higher education, especially scientific education, created a surplus of well-trained scientists, engineers and technicians just when the Internet and telecommunications booms and the year 2000 problem produced a massive need for these professionals in the West. Still more providentially, excess U.S demand for programmers developed just when a critical number of Indian expatriates who had migrated to the US had become chief executive officers and senior executive officers at American technology companies.' Definitely the conditions that prepared the Indian Diaspora to become major contributors to India's technological leap-frogging experience do not exist in Africa today for reasons discussed in earlier sections.

---

[51] For example, the initial postgraduate programmes in public policy and administration at the University of Namibia, Ghana Institute of Public Administration, Uganda Management Institute and the Institute of Public Administration in Mozambique between 1999 and 2005 were started and run jointly by local staff and the African staff at the Institute of Social Studies in The Hague.

[52] Under the WTO General Agreement on Trade in Services liberalisation covers education services at all levels from early childhood development to higher education and in developed countries there are knowledge workers of African origin at all these levels.

The second modality outlined by Kuznetsov (2006) is that of attracting Diaspora members to invest in their former countries. Tracing the history of the so-called 'bamboo network', he explains how the Chinese Diaspora in East and South-East Asia have helped China and Taiwan to acquire and master technologies once dominant in developed countries, but the conditions that have facilitated that process, such as a strong culture of risk taking, an unfaltering attachment to the home country and a policy framework that deliberately established incentives for the Chinese Diaspora to invest in China (Kuznetsov and Sabel 2007: 13-14; Young and Shih, 2003), do not exist at the same level in African countries except perhaps for Egypt, Nigeria, Senegal and South Africa. Basic outsourcing, as a third mechanism, has been used by Armenia, while Korea and China designed policies that managed to attract the physical relocation or return of talented members of the Diaspora (a fourth mechanism) and the conditions for these strategies are beginning to take shape in Africa as the policy and governance reforms take root and policy dialogue on involving the Diaspora begins to produce new thinking. Two more strategies have begun being experimented with in Africa. They include inviting the Diaspora to identify entry points and steer the processes of linking local businesses and investors outside the continent, and encouraging members of the Diaspora to return on short visits and participate in business management, teaching or research. There are many networks linking African HEIs with professionals in the Diaspora. Below are summarised, *some* of the dynamic experiences in selected institutions and countries.

7.1. The South African Network of Skills Abroad: Initiated by University of Cape Town

The South African Network of Skills Abroad (SANSA) was established by the Science and Technology Policy Research Centre at the University of Cape Town in 1998. It aims at attracting the South African scientific and technological Diaspora abroad and connecting them with local scientists, technologists and entrepreneurs in South Africa. Alumni of South African universities living abroad and other skilled South Africans abroad are targeted. By 2002, the network had 2,259 members in more than 60 countries and over 50% of these were South Africans (Kutnetzsov and Sabel 2006: 18). After successful incubation of the network, SANSA was taken over by the National Research Foundation in October 2000.In its new place however, SANSA is not as dynamic as it was when it was under the University of Cape Town.

7.2. The South African Diaspora Network: Founded by the University of Cape Town

This is a mentoring network started by the Centre for Innovation and Entrepreneurship at the University of Cape Town in 2001 with the support of the

World Bank. It seeks to develop mentoring partnerships between South African firms and successful enterprises in the UK, using well-connected business people and policy makers in both countries as brokers. It has about 60 South African businesses and 40 UK enterprises as members involved in exchange of skills and products (Kutnetzsov and Sabel 2007: 18-19).

7.3. Linkages with Experts and Academics in the Diaspora: A Premier Initiative of the Nigerian Universities Commission

Formed in 2007, the Linkages with Experts and Academics in the Diaspora (LEAD), aims at attracting experts and academicians of Nigerian origin in the Diaspora to contribute to the development of Nigerian universities. The major objectives of the programme are:
- To encourage relocation of targeted experts to Nigeria on short-terms basis;
- To tap human resources within and outside the university system for improvement of delivery of university education;
- To encourage easy mobility of staff resources across universities in Nigeria; and
- To encourage experts in industry in Nigeria to participate in teaching in universities.

The terms of the programme are very attractive. They include an economy class ticket, free accommodation, programme related costs and a salary of US$ 1250 - 1750 per month untaxed (Nigerian Universities Commission (NUC): Call for Applications June, 2007). The LEAD initiative adds a new interesting aspect to the idea of linking within knowledge networks. It targets internal and external experts. This raises the issue of the internal Diaspora. These are highly qualified people who have not migrated, but have been pushed to the fringes of the development process either by political factors, economic mismanagement, poor human resources planning, ethnic, gender and racial biases or people identified by Obanya (2004:185-6) whose potential has remained untapped or unutilised or those prematurely retired from the public service. NUC seeks to make a difference by bringing the internal Diaspora back into the education development process.

7.4. Global Educational Initiative for Nigeria

The Global Educational Initiative for Nigeria (GEIFON) is a global knowledge network, which runs a Visiting Lecture Team Programme –International Brain Research Organisation (VLTP-IBRO). It offers courses in areas where capacity is limited in Nigeria. Led by Professor Anthony Ebeige, a physiologist, by June 2007, it had organised two specialised courses on neurological science in collaboration with the Universities of Benin and Lagos. VLTP-IBRO has membership of specialists from the Brazil, Italy, Nigeria, UK and US. It has managed to secure funding from within and outside Nigeria and its partners in Nigeria include the Education Trust Fund, University of Lagos, University of Benin, the Psychiatric Hospital of Usebu in Benin city, Sea Petroleum and Gas Ltd, Ristol Petroleum and Gas Ltd and Nestle Food (Nigeria). (GEIFON June 2007).

These initiatives are a few of the numerous efforts being made by African institutions of higher education, national higher education regulatory agencies and regional higher education networks. The efforts reveal a few things that need emphasis. First, there exist several knowledge networks of willing partners for higher education development that have been active, but links with them are not yet properly and structurally organised to make them focused and sustainable. The US State Department supported Fulbright Fellowship Programme is one of them. It could be more structured and built into initiatives for linking with the Diaspora. Another knowledge network that is actively involved in the higher education programmes of African tertiary education institutions is the Global Development Network through the African Economic Research Consortium (AERC) and the Economic Research Foundation (ERF). There is a need for more structural links between the AAU and AERC, ERF and African Virtual Library (AVU). Third, is the global network of black mathematicians. While the network of black women mathematicians is already working closely with the African Association of Women Mathematicians, there is a need to widen links with the whole network of mathematicians of African affiliation or origins. The AAU could organised a special forum for all listed and unlisted mathematicians of African origin and enable them to find ways of involving the Diaspora in strengthening computer and mathematical sciences on the continent.

Finally, the initiatives by the University of Cape Town, Nigerian Universities Commission and the Global Education Initiative for Nigeria used above, are exemplary attempts to link African higher education institutions with the internal and external Diaspora. Such initiatives deserve support from national, regional and international higher education networks. The existence of these networks indicates that the reservations of the past about the intentions of the Diaspora on Africa and their role are disappearing and being replaced by a new awareness that they are genuine partners, they are keen to give back to the continent that has lost a lot of resources including them, and that if the continent fails to embrace them, they will still come in the service of organisations from the developed countries whose intentions may be to compete with rather to strengthen them. This new awareness needs to be given space in all fora and policy dialogue processes on higher education, including the COREVIP in Tripoli in October 2007 and the ADEA Bi-annual Conference in Maputo in February 2008.

8.0.   Linking Up With Other Global Knowledge Networks

The emergence of regional research and graduate teaching programmes such as those organised by the African Economic Research Consortium has introduced a broader dimension of Africa's participation in global knowledge networks. Therefore, as Ndulu (2004:79) has rightly observed, regional networks will continue to provide the forum for peer review, gateways to global knowledge networks, effective means for specialised training and enhanced recognition of African intellectual development processes and outcomes. This section examines the role and potential of two types of networks. First, the global and regional networks for knowledge sharing and second, the global and regional Diaspora networks. While there are many global knowledge networks that have contributed substantially to capacity development in the region, this section focuses on three: the Global Development Network, Fulbright Fellows Programme and the network of black mathematicians.

8.1.   The Global Development Network

This is one of the most widely operational networks for collaborative teaching and research in the social sciences, with members on all continents and specialising in graduate programmes and global collaborative and competitive research programmes. It is a North – South knowledge-sharing partnership. Its member institutions include the African Economic Research Consortium (AERC), one of the most prestigious networks on economic research and training in the region based in Nairobi, the Eastern European Economic Research Institute Network (CERGE) in Prague, the East Asian Development Research Network (EADN) in Bangkok, the Mediterranean Economic Research Foundation (ERF) in Cairo, the Economics Education and Research Consortium (EERC) in Moscow, the European Development Research Network (EUDN) in Brussels, the Organisation for Development Research Network (ODN) in Port Moresby, and the South Asian Network for Economic Research Institutes (SANEI) in Islamabad.[53]

The resources of the network include Internet-based resources at the ERF in Cairo, funds for research with a portfolio of close to US $20 million accessible on competitive basis, an extensive mentoring, peer review and workshop programme, and a membership of over 3700 scholars in 95 countries in the North and South. The network organises research competitions and awards medals for excellent and innovative research. It organises activities aimed at enabling access to global knowledge[54], communicating local knowledge[55] and building partnerships for local

---

[53] Based on GDN presentation posted on the web at File:///c:/Documents%20and 20%settings/MPPA/Local%20settings/Temporary downloaded on the 2nd October 2007 at 10 am.

knowledge.[55] Although the AERC and ERF have been very active in facilitating resource sharing among African universities and global systems of knowledge, their potential has not been exhausted. Their links with several tertiary education institutions and networks are still weak or non-existent and they should be brought closer to the networks such as the AAU and sub-regional organisations.

8.2.   The Fulbright Fellowship Programme

This is one of the oldest and most effective US-based programmes that links scholars globally and has been very active in capacity development for African universities over a long time. Although it links academics from all backgrounds to all countries and universities globally, in this report its importance lies more in its contribution to linking the African universities with the African Diaspora in the US. In the next section, we shall examine more closely the emerging role of the Diaspora in African higher education development. In the table below are shown the total number of fellows of African origin that came to African universities under the programme from 1999 to Mid-2007. A total of 279 such experts came as visiting fellows during this period. About 50% were of social sciences background, although another good number came for research and teaching in management, engineering, sciences and medicine.

The most popular destinations of the group were South Africa, Ghana, Nigeria, Senegal, Egypt, Zimbabwe and Botswana, Morocco and Tunisia in that order. The adequate funding of universities in terms of facilities for teaching and research accounts for the popularity of the countries in the two cones of the continent, while historical ties and the systematic efforts to keep in touch with alumni and Diaspora networks by the university leaders in West Africa, help to increase the popularity of the three West African countries as a popular destinations. It is clear however, that the potential for the Fulbright Fellowship Programme to become a stronger rallying point for Diaspora networking is very high, although this factor has not been given the emphasis it deserves by higher education development partners in the region.

See www.gdnet.org/online-services
www.gdnet.org/development-research
Www.gdnet.org/regional-windows

Table 2: Fulbright Fellows of African Origin 1999-2007 by Disciplines

Country	Total Number	Agric Sciences	Engineering & Geology	Maths	Sciences	IT & Information	Arts	Management	Medicine & Health
Algeria	1				1				
Benin	6	1		1			3		
Botswana	13	1	3		2	2	2		3
Burkina Faso	2						2		
Cameroon	6				1		3	1	1
Chad	1				1				
Cote divorce	2	1					1		
DRC	1						1		
Egypt	13	1	3				5	2	2
Eritrea	1						1		
Ethiopia	9	1	2		1		4	1	
Gambia	2						2		
Ghana	32	1	1		2	2	21	5	
Guinea	4						4		
Kenya	3						3		
Madagascar	2						2		
Malawi	4						4		
Mali	4						3	1	
Mauritius	3	1	2						
Morocco	9	1	2			1	2	3	
Mozambique	8				1	1	2	3	1
Namibia	12	1	1			2	6		2
Niger	1						1		
Nigeria	22		2		1	2	10	5	2
Rwanda	1								1
Senegal	10		1				8	1	
South Africa	71	5	3	1	8	3	36	10	5
Swaziland	3	1					1	1	
Tanzania	5	1				1	2	1	
Togo	1								1
Tunisia	5		1				1	2	1
Uganda	6				1		2		3
Zambia	3				1	1			1
Zimbabwe	13	1	1		1		6	2	1
Total	279	17	22	2	21	15	136	38	24

8.3.   Global Networks of Mathematicians in Africa and the Diaspora

Another important knowledge network that deserves attention for African universities is that of mathematicians of African or black origin. This network has two faces. First, is the network of black women mathematicians that works closely with Association of African Women Mathematicians.[57]   The list of people in the network is attached as Appendix 3. Equally important is the knowledge network of black mathematicians. In Appendix 4 is a list of top black mathematician based in Africa, Europe and North America, who have published international quality articles on mathematical issues. In the table below, their geographical distribution is indicated.

Table 3:   Regional Distribution of Top Black Mathematicians Registered By the American Mathematics Society by September 2007

Country or region	Number
US and Canada	83
Europe	14
Caribbean	5
Latin America	2
Benin	1
Burkina Faso	1
Cameroon	5
Congo	1
Egypt	1
Gabon	1
Kenya	1
Lesotho	1
Niger	1
Nigeria	14
Senegal	5
South Africa	3
Zimbabwe	3
Total Bas ed in Africa	*38*
Grand Total	**142**

Search the web for black women in mathematics research

From the list, it can be noted that while the majority lives in developed countries, some live on the continent and all are Africans. Their names, as indicated on the appended list, can be used to establish links with them as they can be traced through search engines. These provide another potential network of experts who it would be interesting for African universities to work with. With intensified efforts to coordinate them and provide them with a special forum, these mathematicians, some of whom live on the African continent, can constitute a dynamic transformational force in mathematics and computer science.

9.0.   Conclusions

Through curriculum, organizational and financial reforms, higher education institutions have embarked on a long and tiresome path of institutional change and renewal. As they increase the pace of reforms, they may be able to bring themselves closer to the changes going on at regional and global level. They may subsequently bridge the gap between their goals and the means to achieve them. In the process of change, they face a variety of challenges that need to be addressed. Some of these include relevance of curricula and research programmes; quality of courses and research output; visibility among partners and potential customers; the pace and rhythm of internal decision making processes; strategic leadership for resource mobilisation, motivating staff and obtaining the best results out of existing resources; programme development and management; performance measurement and effective management of activities and resources; accountability and institutional integrity; development of norms and systems for measuring outputs and outcomes and internal and external networking.

The readiness of regional bodies and international development partners to support higher education on the continent is unmistakable. ADEA has pioneered funding of research networks and studies on various areas including teacher training programmes, HIV/AIDS, gender and institutional change and now staff retention. The Partnership for Higher Education in Africa is also increasing its support for interventions on quality assurance, IT, leadership development and innovation systems in HEIs. Bilateral development partners are addressing specific issues including funding research, partnerships in collaborative programmes, staff development and institution building. Regional bodies are also increasing their role and involvement in higher education issues. The African Capacity Building Foundation has committed itself to strengthening training at postgraduate level on public sector management and provided funds for common programmes of HEIs through the AAU. The African Development Bank is finalising its Higher Education Science and Technology programme that is intended to target special initiatives of African HEIs in the effort to revitalise higher education on the continent. The AU Plan of Action for the second Decade on Education seeks, among other things, to revitalise higher education and gives the AAU a coordinating role on higher education initiatives.

The current situation creates the necessary conditions for partnerships between HEIs and their governments, development partners and various sectors at national level, on the one hand, and regional higher education organisations, national higher education bodies and international development agencies, on the other, for concerted efforts to rejuvenate higher education, support the contribution of HEIs to economic development and to help the African countries to become participants in the brain exchange on the international labour market instead of remaining net exporters of skilled professionals to other countries and advanced economies. Below are some recommendations on what each of the partners can contribute to these efforts.

10. Recommendations

10.1. Recommendations to Higher Education Institutions

Strengthening teaching and learning
a. Strengthen internal quality assurance systems through self-assessment, peer review, and regular voluntary programme accreditation.
b. Introduce customer surveys, student involvement in evaluation of courses and ensure customer follow-up.
c. Institutionalise customer or stakeholder contact through focus groups in key institutions, listed contacts and electronic feedback mechanisms.
d. Introduce academic quality guarantees and spot-check procedures and enforcement mechanisms, sanctions and rewards.
e. Develop lifelong learning programmes for academic and administrative staff and strengthen human resources management.

Improving research management
a. Develop long-term research programmes on issues relevant to national development programmes and long-term national development visions and goals.
b. Strengthen partnerships with governments and the private sector.
c. Increase inter-faculty, multi-disciplinary collaborative research.
d. Increase transparency in programmes and resources accruing from research and technical advisory services.

Staff recruitment and advancement
a. Devolve recruitment and promotion procedures to colleges and faculties, while retaining quality control functions at the centre.
b. Shorten time taken in decision-making on recruitment and promotion in the context of competition for skills within and outside national borders.

Diversifying financial resources
c. Enter into partnerships with the private sector for research and provision of

services.

d. Increase earnings from research contracts from private sector and governments.
e. Negotiate franchises with state-owned enterprises for product development and service provision.
f. Commercialise innovations and intellectual property arising out of research.
g. Strengthen statistical and data systems and develop quantitative and qualitative norms for inputs, outputs and outcomes in all core activities.

Linking with the Diaspora

a. Establish or strengthen links with alumni within and outside national boarders and establish databases on their areas of specialisation.
b. Identify areas where the Diaspora can have a value-added contribution to make and link them up with relevant faculties and departments.
c. Develop joint programmes with Diaspora organisations for funding and support for Diaspora involvement in selected areas.

10.2. Recommendations to national authorities

a. Increase training on higher education management, quality assurance and leadership for change management in higher education institutions and support education reforms.
b. Develop norm-based funding formulae for all education sectors.
c. Upgrade norms for quality assessment in all sectors of education.
d. Address factors that affect the quality of education at all levels.
e. Develop sound systems for managing statistics, data and information on education sectors, especially higher education.
f. Decentralise decision making on staff travel, recruitment and promotion to institutions of higher education to reduce delays or loss of staff caused by lengthy procedures.
g. Reduce bottlenecks on education staff travel, visa and employment permits within the region.
h. Negotiate with developed countries for restriction of recruitment in sectors at risk in African countries such as health and education.
i. Develop codes of conduct on foreign recruitment in sectors at risk within national borders.
j. Encourage voluntary codes of social responsibility for multinational corporations and foreign higher education bodies operating within national borders on recruitment and transfer of staff to home countries or offices in other countries or regions.
k. Increase public awareness about the role the Diaspora can play in revitalising higher education and the African economies and develop systems to support the involvement of the Diaspora in this process.
l. Improve capacity for implementing regional and international commitments.

10.3. Recommendations to regional bodies and international development partners

a. Improve coordination of support and interventions by working through a few designated bodies at regional level, thereby reducing duplication of efforts and maximising outcomes.

b. Develop a division of tasks that ensures each actor specialises in an area that matches their experience and interests to avoid concentration in same areas and neglect of other areas.

c. Combine efforts to ensure the enforcement of codes of conduct developed by the EU and several OECD countries restricting recruitment in sectors at risk in developing countries.

d. Support the development of capacity for policy management, analysis, implementation and innovation at national and regional level.

e. Develop common frameworks on funding research including promoting demand-driven research programmes, reducing support for individualised research and promoting transparency and accountability for research results and outcomes.

f. Support sandwich staff development programmes in order to strengthen capacity for local training and making training and research more relevant to the region.

g. Intensify support for IT and computer-based research and teaching methods in African HEIs.

References

AAU, ADEA Working Group on Higher Education 2004, *Higher Education Innovations in Sub-Saharan Africa*, Association of African Universities, Accra.

Abangi, O., 2003, 'Revitalizing Financing of Higher Education in Kenya: Resource Utilization in Public Universities' in J. Babalola and B.O Emunemu, (Eds.) 2003, *Issues in Higher Education: Research Evidence From Sub-Sahara Africa*, National Universities Commission (NUC) Nigeria, Association of African Universities, and Higher Education Research Policy Network (HERNET), University of Ibadan, pp.157-185

Appelton, S., 2001, 'Education, Incomes and Poverty in Uganda in the 1990s', Centre for Research in Development and International Trade (CREDIT), University of Nottingham, Credit Research Paper No. 01/22, www.nottinghm.ac.uk/economics/ researc/credit.

AU, 2004, 'Report of the First Conference of Intellectuals of Africa and the Diaspora' First Conference of Intellectuals of Africa and the Diaspora, 6-9 October 2004, Dakar, Senegal, Document AU/Rpt/CAID (I),

Babalola, J.B, A.O. Jaiyeoba and O. Okediran, 2003, 'University Autonomy and Financial Reforms in Nigeria: Historical Background, Issues and Recommendations from Experience', in J. Babalola and B.O Emunemu, (Eds.) 2003, *Issues in Higher Education: Research Evidence From Sub-Sahara Africa*, National Universities Commission (NUC) Nigeria, Association of African Universities, and Higher Education Research Policy Network (HERNET), University of Ibadan.pp.297-324.

Barnett, R., 2000, 'University knowledge in the age of supercomplexity' in *Higher Education* 40: 409-422

Becher, T., 1989, 'Historians on history', in *Studies in Higher Education*, 14(3), 263-278

Blair, R. and J. Jordan, 1994, *Staff Loss and Retention at Selected African Universities: A Synthesis Report*, AFTHR, Technical Note No.18, Human Resources and Poverty Division, Technical Department, Africa Region, Washington DC, World Bank.

Butare, A., 2004, 'Income generating Activities in Higher Education: the Case of Kigali Institute of Science and Technology and Management (KIST)', in *Journal of Higher Education in Africa,* Volume 2, Number 3, 2004, pp.37-54

Clark, B., 1998, *Creating Entrepreneurial Universities,* Oxford, Pergamon

Clark, B., 2004, 'Delienating the character of the Entrepreneurial University', in *Higher Education Policy,* 2004, 17:355-370.

Crush, J., W.Pendelton and D.S. Tevera, 2005, *Degrees of Uncertainty: Students and The Brain Drain in Southern Africa,* Southern African Migration Project, Cape Town.

Dovlo, D., 2004, 'The Brain Drain in Africa: An Emerging Challenge to Health Professionals', Education' in *Journal of Higher Education in Africa,* Volume 2, Number 3, 2004, pp.1-18.

ECA 1999, African Development Forum '99 Meeting Summary, 'The Role of African Digital Diaspora in Enhancing ICT Development in Africa' September 13-19 1999 on http://www.undp.org/tcdc/index2.html

Ekong, D, and .A. Sawyerr 1999, *Higher Education Leadership in Africa. A Case Book,* Maskew Miller/Longman, Cape Town.

Enos, J.L., 1995, *In pursuit of science and technology in Sub-Saharan Africa. The impact of structural adjustment programmes,* Routledge, London and New York

Findlay, A., 2002, 'From Brain Exchange to Brain Gain: Policy Implications for the UK of Recent Trends in Skilled Migration From Developing Countries' ILO International Migration Papers, No .43, at p.20

GEIFON, 2007, 'Report on IBRO Neuroscience Course, University of Lagos, Nigeria, July18-26, 2007' University of Lagos, mimeo.

Goldstein, A, and C.Kauffmann, 'African Economic Outlook 2005/2006', *Policy Insights* No. 21, OECD Development Centre.

Hall .M , A.Symes and T. Luescher, 2004, *The Governance Merger in South African Higher Education, Research Report* prepared for the Council of Higher Education, Council on Higher Education, Pretoria.

Hargrieves, A., and P. Shaw, 2005, 'Knowledge and Skill Development in Developing and Transitional Economy. An Analysis of World Bank / DFiD Knowledge and Skills for the Modern Economy Project' (mimeo)

Ishengoma, M.J., 2004, 'CostSharing in Higher Education in Tanzania: Fact or Fiction?', in *Journal of Higher Education in Africa*, Volume 2, Number 2, 2004, pp.101-134.

Ishengoma, M.J., 2007, 'International Brain Drain and Its Impact on Higher Education Institutions' Capacity Building and Human Resources Development in Sub-Saharan Africa: The Case of Tanzania' in Association of African Universities, *The African Brian Drain-Managing the Drain: Working with the Diaspora, Conference of Rectors, Vice Chancellors and Presidents, 2007, Papers*, 21-25 October, Tripoli Libya, pp. 11-21

IOM, 2000, Conference Report on, "Orderly Migration-Visions and Challenges for the 21st Century" On the occasion of the 10th Anniversary of the IOM Mission in the Netherlands, 5 November 2001, p.27

Johnstone, D., 2004, 'Higher Education Finance and Accessibility: Tuition Fees and Student Loans in Sub-Saharan Africa', in *Journal of Higher Education in Africa*, Volume 2, Number 2, 2004, pp.11-36.

Kekäle, J., 2000, 'Quality assessment in diverse disciplinary settings' in *Higher Education*, 40: 465-488.

Kauffmann, C., N. Pinnaud and L. Wegner, 2006, 'African Economic Outlook 2006.A Two Sped Continent', *Policy Insights*, No. 22, OECD Development Centre.

Kenneth Prewitt, 2004, 'Higher Education, Society and Government: Changing Dynamics', in *Journal of Higher Education in Africa*, Volume 2, No.1, 2004

Kiamba, C., 2004, 'Privately Sponsored Students and Other Income Generating Activities at the University of Nairobi', in *Journal of Higher Education in Africa*, Volume 2, Number 2, 2004, pp.53-74.

Kuznetsov, Y., 2006, 'International Migration of Talent and Home Country Development: Towards and Virtuous Cycle', Paper presented at *Seminario Promoviendo Redes Innovacio Para Desarraolo Y El Empleo*, organized at the World Bank Institute, Washington DC.

Kuznetsov, Y., and C. Sabel, 2007, 'Work Globally, Develop Locally: Diaspora Networks as Springboards of KnowledgeBased Development', in *Innovation, Management, Policy and Practice* 8(1-2).

Logue, Danielle, 2007, 'The Role of Universities in Managing Scientific Mobility: A Study of institutional Pressures for Change at Global level' in Association of African Universities, *The African Brian Drain-Managing the Drain: Working with the Diaspora, Conference of Rectors, Vice Chancellors and Presidents, 2007, Papers*, 21-25 October, Tripoli Libya, pp. 72-80

Martin Hall, Ashley Symes and Thierry Luescher, 2004, *The Governance of Merger in South African Higher Education. Research Report Prepared for the Council on Higher Education*, Council on Higher Education, Pretoria.

Mayanja, M.K., 2005, 'Privatization, Internationalization and the Implications of GATS for Higher Education in Africa: The Case of Uganda', in Association of African Universities, *Conference Papers*, 11th AAU General Conference 21-25 February, 2005, pp. 219-250.

Maclure, R., 1997, *Overlooked and Undervalued. A Synthesis of ERNWACA Reviews on the State of Education Research in West and Central Africa*, Educational Research Network for West and Central Africa (ERNWACA), Support for Analysis and Research in Africa (SARA), Health and Human Resources Analysis for Africa (HHRAA) and US Agency for International Development.

Marfouk, A., 2007, 'African Brian Drain: Scope and Determinants' in Association of African Universities, *The African Brian Drain-Managing the Drain: Working with the Diaspora, Conference of Rectors, Vice Chancellors and Presidents, 2007, Papers*, 21-25 October, Tripoli Libya, pp. 98-128

Mihyo, Paschal B., 2004, 'GATS and Higher Education in Africa: Conceptual Issues and Development Perspectives', in Association of African Universities, *The Implications of WTO/GATS for Higher Education*, AAU, Accra.

Mihyo, Paschal B., 2006, 'Quality Assurance in Higher Education in Tanzania' Paper submitted to the World Bank as part of a six country study of quality assurance in African universities.

Moharir, V., 2003, 'Governance and Policy Analysis' in D. Olowu and S. Sako, ((Eds.), *Better Governance and Public Policy in Africa*, Kumarian Press, Bloomfield, pp. 107-124

Musisi, N.B and Muwanga N.K, 2003, *Makerere University in Transition 1993-2000*, Partnership for Higher Education in Africa, James Curry Oxford and Fountain Publishers, Kampala.

Ndulu, B.J., 2004, 'Human Capital Flight: Stratification, Globalization, and the Challenges to Tertiary Education in Africa' in *Journal Higher Education in Africa*, Volume 2, No.1 2004, pp.57-92

Niles, F.S., 1998, 'IndividualismCollectivism Revisited' in *Cross-Cultural Research* **32**: 315-341

Obanya, P., 2004, *Educating for the Knowledge Economy*, Mauro Publishers, Ibadan.

Omari, I., and P.B. Mihyo, 1991, *The Roots of Student Unrest in African Universities*, IDRC, Nairobi.

Otieno, W., 2004, 'Student Loans in Kenya: Past Experiences, Current Hurdles, and Opportunities for the Future', in *Journal of Higher Education in Africa*, Volume 2, Number 2, 2004, pp.75-100.

Pillay, P., 2004, "The South African Experience with Developing and Implementing a Funding Formula for the Tertiary Education System', in *Journal of Higher Education in Africa*, Volume 2, Number 3, 2004, pp.19-36.

Nakabo-Ssewanyana, S., 1999, 'Statistical Data: The Underestimated Tool for Higher Education Management: the Case of Makerere University', in *Higher Education*, 37:259-279

Nakabo-Ssewanyana, S., 2003, 'Statistical Data: The Underestimated Tool for Higher Education Management : the Case of Makerere University', in J. Babalola and B.O Emunemu, (Eds.) 2003, *Issues in Higher Education: Research Evidence From Sub-Sahara Africa*, National Universities Commission (NUC) Nigeria, Association of African Universities, and Higher Education Research Policy Network (HERNET), University of Ibadan, pp.273-296

Sawyerr, A., 2002, 'Challenges Facing African Universities: Selected Issues', on http:www.africanstudies.org/challengesFacingAfricanUniversities.pdf

Sawyerr, A., 2004, 'Challenges Facing African Universities: Selected Issue' *African Studies Review*, Volume 47, Number 1 (April 2004), pp.1-59

Schmid, M., 2007 'Courting the Masterminds -The European Union's Efforts to Attract Researchers' in *Bridges* Vol.15, September 2007/Letter from Brussels, on http://www.ostina.org downloaded 29/09/2007.

Shabani, J., 2004, 'Regional Convention for the Recognition of Studies and Degrees of Higher Education in Africa', in Association of African Universities, *The Implications of WTO/GATS for Higher Education*, AAU, Accra

Shah, R., 2007, ' Report on Global Health, Justice and the Brain Drain Conference', in Association of African Universities, *The African Brian Drain-Managing the Drain: Working with the Diaspora, Conference of Rectors, Vice Chancellors and Presidents, 2007, Papers*, 21-25 October, Tripoli Libya, pp. 61-71.

Teal, F., 2001, 'Education, Incomes, Poverty and Inequality in Ghana in the 1990s', Centre for the Study of African Economies (CESAE), University of Oxford, CESAE Working Paper Series 2001-21

Tettey, W., 2006, 'Staff Retention in African Universities: Elements of a Sustainable Strategy', Report Submitted to the World Bank. Washington DC.

Tevera, D.S., 2005, *Early Departures: The Emigration Potential of Zimbabwean Students*, Southern African Migration Project, Cape Town.

Torres, Rosa Maria, 2004, *Lifelong Learning in the South: Critical Issues and Opportunities for Adult Education*, Sida Studies No.11, Sida, Stockholm.

Triandis, H.C., 1995, *Individualism and Collectivism*, Boulder, Co, Wetview

UNESCO, 2002, EFA Global Monitoring Report, *Education for All. Is the World on Track?* UNESCO, Paris

UNESCO, 2003/4, EFA Global Monitoring Report, Gender and Education for All. THE LEAP TO EQUALITY, UNESCO, Paris.

Woodhall, M., 2004, 'Student Loans: Potential, Problems and Lessons from International Experience', in *Journal of Higher Education in Africa*, Volume 2, Number 2, 2004, pp.37-52.

Young, N., and J. Shih, 2003, 'The Chinese Diaspora and Philanthropy', paper Commissioned by the Global Equity Initiative, Harvard University.

ANNEXES (Other Annexes are in Volume II of the Report)

Annex 1:   **Officials Interviewed**

Ghana Institute of Management and Public Administration
- Prof. Agyeman Badu, Deputy Rector

Kigali Institute of Science, Technology and Management
- Mr. Gerard Nyabutsitsi, Deputy Rector –Administration and Finance
- Ms. Mukalinda, Human Resources Manager
- Mr. Papias Musafiri, Head of management Department

Kwame Nkrumah University of Science and Technology
- Prof. Kwasi Kwafo Adarkwa, Vice Chancellor
- Prof. W.O Ellis, Pro-Vice Chancellor

National University of Rwanda
- Prof. Hebert Nsanze, Dean– Faculty of Medicine.
- Ms. Gloriosa Mwizirigimva, Human Resources Manager
- Mr. Patrick Kitayezu, Human Resources Development Officer
- Mr. Simeon Sebatukura, Permanent Secretary– Annual Organizations
- Mr. Jovin Akaana-Shenge, Administrative Officer– Faculty of Medicine.

University of Cape Coast, Ghana
- Prof. Odow-Obeng, Vice Chancellor
- Mr. Kofi Ohene, Registrar
- Ms. Sika Akoto, Centre of International Education

University of Ghana
- Prof. Eric Danquah, Dean International Programmes
- Prof. Lante Lawson, Dean School of Medicine
- Prof. Nii Otu, Provost, Dental School

University of Zambia
- Prof. Stephen Simukanga, Vice Chancellor
- Dr. A.N Ng'andu, Registrar
- Ms. Theresa L. M. Sichilongo, Deputy Registrar
- Prof Oliver Saasa, Executive Director– Premier Consultant
- Ms. C.M Wonani, Department of Development Studies